MW01009053

What Others Are Saying About
Becoming a Woman of Spiritual Passion

Blending personal fervor for her Lord, theological scholarship, and suggestions for practical application, Donna Morley challenges her readers to cultivate an appetite for the things of God. The book's contagious content inspires women to eagerly embark on a lifestyle that is motivated by spiritual passion.

Pat Ennis, Professor, Department of Home Economics,
The Master's College, Co-author of *Becoming a Woman Who Pleases God*

Donna Morley accurately shines the spotlight of truth onto the cause and cure for our spiritual dullness—she challenges and inspires women to do whatever it takes to become passionate about Christ. This is a life-changing, must-read book!

Christine D. Anderson
Editor, LifeWay Christian Resources

As a Christian radio talk-show host and speaker I read numerous books a month to keep myself current with the life events, trends, and passions of my listening audiences. Donna Morley's *Becoming a Woman of Spiritual Passion* captured my attention as she shared from her heart, provoked my emotions with the spiritually affirming life experiences of others, and tied everything together with the rich truths of Scripture. This is a practical must-read for any woman who desires to "walk the walk" and become a spiritually passionate daughter of our glorious heavenly Father.

Linda Goldfarb
Founder of the Not Just Talkin' the Talk Ministries
Syndicated talk radio host, speaker, writer

How do we deepen our relationship with the Lord.

Donna Morley exposes the inexplicable joy of belonging to Jesus in mind, body, and spirit. With refreshing ease, she removes the last barriers to wholly surrendering to Christ and guides the way with stories and examples that remin us of ourselves and allow us to see hope.

My work with women in traumatic and crisis living shows many women are turning to the ways of the world for help instead of to the promises found in God's Word. Donna Morley provides women with the essentials for building a truly life-changing relationship with God. I am thrilled to have this resource.

Bev Trusting — Faith   Ryan & Lori

Ch. 7 —

Jace Rembering / Calling —
Scripture   Prayer, *Scripture

Brad Enduring —

BECOMING
A WOMAN OF
SPIRITUAL
PASSION

DONNA MORLEY

HARVEST HOUSE PUBLISHERS

EUGENE, OREGON

Cover by Koechel Peterson & Associates, Inc., Minneapolis, Minnesota

BECOMING A WOMAN OF SPIRITUAL PASSION
Copyright © 2005 by Donna Morley
Published by Harvest House Publishers
Eugene, Oregon 97402
www.harvesthousepublishers.com

Library of Congress Cataloging-in-Publication Data
Morley, Donna, 1959-
Becoming a woman of spiritual passion / Donna Morley.
    p. cm.
ISBN-13: 978-0-7369-1579-3
ISBN-10: 0-7369-1579-6 (pbk.)
1. Christian women—Religious life. I. Title
BV4527.M64 2005
248.8'43—dc22   2005001907

Printed in the United States of America

    05 06 07 08 09 10 11 12 13 / BP-MS / 10 9 8 7 6 5 4 3 2 1

Daughter—
an ordinary word, used by billions of people.
Like so many lovely and precious things,
the word can become tarnished by fading character.
But, when I speak of
Michelle Morley as my *daughter,*
I use the word with the utmost pride.
She is rare, like a priceless jewel.

I love you Michelle,
and am proud of the woman you are becoming.
"Continue in the grace of God" (Acts 13:43).

Acknowledgments

I hope the reader will bear with me as I thank some very special people, starting with my dear friends who consistently prayed for me and sent notes of encouragement. I won't list you all here, but you know I am speaking directly to you. I love you, and thank God for bringing you into my life!

I have been just as blessed by all my friends at Harvest House, who have been so overwhelmingly supportive. I am most appreciative to president Bob Hawkins, Jr., whose excitement, supportiveness, and belief that this project is indeed important to women in the church was fuel for the flame as I wrote. Thank you, Bob!

Speaking of writing...just as a book cannot be judged by its cover, so a writer can't be judged completely on his or her own merit. It takes a team to write a book, and an important part of that team is the editor. I'm thankful to the Lord for giving me Steve Miller. He worked tirelessly on this book, making it shine like gold. Thank you, Steve!

I am also thankful and undeserving of my loving family. Despite his own book deadline, my husband, Brian, dropped everything to read my entire manuscript and offer suggestions that helped make some of my points clearer. I am also thankful for his prayers and those of my children, Michelle and Johnathan. How often Johnathan would remind me, "Mom, I'm praying for you *lots!*" Thank you Brian, Michelle, and Johnathan for your supportiveness and love.

Lastly, thank You, dear Lord, for Your pure and living Word (Psalm 12:6), which moves hearts; for Your example (Matthew 11:29; 1 Peter 2:21), which helps us in our daily journey; and for Your passion (Jeremiah 33:3; Habakkuk 1:5), which motivates and excites us to discover great things from You. Without these things I certainly couldn't have written this book. Help me and every reader to continually learn from You. Allow our cup to overflow with all that is spiritual and that comes from You.

Now we have received, not the spirit of the world,
but the Spirit who is from God,
that we may know the things freely given to us by God,
which things we also speak,
not in words taught by human wisdom,
but in those taught by the Spirit,
combining spiritual thoughts with spiritual words....
we have the mind of Christ
(1 Corinthians 2:12-13,16).

Contents

❦

When We Say "I Do" to Jesus 9

Part 1: Your Beloved's Promises

1. The Promise of a Better Future 17

2. The Promise of Protection and Strength 35

3. The Promise of Provision for Your Every Need 59

4. The Promise of an Everlasting Love 77

Part 2: Building Your Passion for Jesus

5. Living Out Your Marriage Vow to Christ 95

6. Deepening the Relationship 113

7. Giving Him All Your Love 129

8. Experiencing Uninterrupted Joy 145

9. Coveting His Love Letters 165

10. Telling Others I Am His, He Is Mine 193

11. Enduring in Total Devotion 213

Appendix: Do You Belong to Jesus? 227

Notes 233

When We Say "I Do" to Jesus

Days after I became a Christian, I felt as though I were flying! It was as if I had literally died and gone to heaven. I wondered how I could have lived for 21 years having never taken to heart such miraculous truths as repentance, forgiveness, and *salvation!*

Oh, in every anxious, hopeful human heart, the question is asked, After death, will I live again? The one called *Life* answers, Yes! for all who come to Him (John 14:6). In the Father's house there is a call that echoes, "Come! Come! Come!" (see Revelation 22:17). This spectacular invitation is to all of us. I still remember the life-changing event when on September 10, 1980, I responded to that heavenly message, and committed myself to Jesus with the words, "I do." *I do* commit my life to Jesus. *I do* come under His rule and authority. *I do* want to follow Him and love Him all the days of my life.

In prayer, I had asked Him to forgive me of my past, present, and future sins—and He graciously did. Because of my new life with Jesus, I turned from living for myself to living for Him. I, who would have been rightly condemned by divine justice, was now accepted by divine grace. On that day I exchanged hell for heaven, and the angels in heaven rejoiced (Luke 15:7). Nothing compares to this experience of spiritual rejuvenation nor the experience of those early days when my devotion to Jesus was unhindered and my praise to Him was unreserved.

While my prayers were directed upward, so too were my thoughts as I contemplated life in heaven for eternity. Imagine. If the word *life* is a comforting word, then *eternal life* is the greatest comfort that can be spoken by human lips. Yet, which one of us can accurately describe it? Yes, we see a glimpse of the heavenly life in Scripture, but as a zealous babe in Christ, I wanted to know everything about it—yet I couldn't. No matter how much knowledge I started to gain from the Bible, I came to see that the full meaning of *eternity* rises so high above us and stretches so far beyond us that we can't fully comprehend it. I surmised, I'll just have to wait until I get to heaven…but I can't wait. The thought of being in the presence of Jesus, face to face, was so marvelous that waiting for heaven seemed unbearable.

How I loved those early days of being born again! I had a million and one questions to ask anyone at church who would patiently help me. And, as I began getting answers, I came to discover some profound spiritual truths—one of which completely surprised me. I found out that anyone who says, "I do" to Jesus has become "*the bride,* the wife of the Lamb" (Revelation 21:9). Prior to becoming a Christian, I thought that only a certain group of women who wore uniforms—or habits, as they call them—were entitled to be called the bride of Christ. But according to the Bible, the bride is the church (Revelation 21:3); and what is the *true church* made up of? Individual saints (male and female) whose names are written in the Lamb's Book of Life (Revelation 21:27), who are "faithful unto death" (Revelation 2:10), and whose purity and faithfulness are symbolized under the figure of the "wife of the Lamb" (Revelation 21:9).

Have you ever thought deeply about what it means to you to be the Lord's bride? When I think about this, it's still hard for me to fathom. You see, had the Lord made such a proclamation to angels, or to the heavenly saints, or to the greatest Christians here on earth, well then that statement would be easier to believe. But to include me—and all believers—as His bride…that completely amazed me!

One day after Sunday service an elderly woman named Josie made a comment that took me aback. I thought about it for a long time. While we were walking slowly toward the exit, she turned to me and said thoughtfully, "Donna, whatever you do, don't ever lose your zeal for Christ."

Puzzled about why she would say such a thing, and not knowing how to reply, I blurted out without thinking, "Certainly not!" I simply couldn't understand how I, or any Christian, could ever lose their passion for the One who loves us so much and rescued us from the horrors of hell.

Unfortunately, after 25 years of living the Christian life, I now understand Josie's haunting admonishment all too well. My passion for Jesus hasn't always seen perpetual sunshine. I have seen how easily my "Hosannas" can diminish from my lips, and how fast my devotion can die. How convicting the words of Jeremiah 2:1, given to Israel, but which can certainly be directed at us: "I remember the devotion of your youth, how as a bride you loved me" (NIV). Notice the word loved in the past tense? The Lord was pointing out that their *passion* for Him was gone.

> Spiritual passion is an appetite and a hunger for the things of God.

Every one of us must ask: Is my passion, my *spiritual passion*, gone? Or, does it come and go? Are there hindrances in my life keeping me from having that passion? Deep in my heart, I long for—and am striving after—a spiritual passion for the long haul, one that outlasts this life.

What Is Spiritual Passion?

Spiritual passion is an appetite and a hunger for the things of God. It yearns to follow Him and live out His will. Far from apathy and coldness, it fosters a heart and life devoted to Christ, desirous to return His love. Such passion and zeal ought to flow from us not out of compulsion, but with warmth and sincerity.

This passion offers our heart, soul, and mind—and our efforts, perseverance, and steadfastness—to the service of Christ. Passion is what turns a struggle into newfound strength, a burden into a blessing, a crisis into a victory.

Spiritual passion is enthusiastic in devotion, in praise, and in prayer. Without compromise, it stands firm, believing intensely that right is mightier than wrong, good more powerful than evil, purity stronger than immorality, and truth greater than error.

Such passion isn't fanatical, lacking in intellect, nor fit for weak minds only. No. It accompanies divine authority and power in which the godly live out a meaningful life to the fullest.

When we cultivate such passion, we join ourselves to a host of others whose hearts have shone brightly for God—cherubim and seraphim, angels and archangels, patriarchs, prophets, apostles, martyrs, reformers, thinkers and scholars of the church, saints in heaven and on earth. It is a passion that unites us with others of like mind and heart and invests in the kingdom of heaven.

Such passion is priceless. Throughout history, spiritual passion has always been the founder of noble causes, reaching out in devotion to Christ, and with love toward others. The human heart is made for this. But when a person is unconnected to God, the passions of the heart run undirected, like a runaway truck with no steering wheel. And absent spiritual direction, people are zealous for the oddest things, such as wanting both to protect whales and abort babies. Other people simply value passion of any kind, as if the sheer experience of it is what matters and not what a person is passionate about.

True spiritual passion—which seeks God and His will—are part of the normal Christian life. Normal here doesn't necessarily mean average in the sense that every Christian has it. But the Christian woman who is walking with God and not blocking the Holy Spirit in her life should have an inward passion. This passion is not emotionalism or sentimentalism;

rather, it is a spiritual energy that seeks to exalt God, minister to others, and refuses to be sidetracked or quenched.

A look behind every godly life will reveal a spiritual passion, however quiet and controlled. Spiritual passion is what separates those who really want what God wants—and want it with their whole being—from those who are merely going through the motions.

Perhaps you have longed to be a woman of spiritual passion, but at times you wonder if it's even possible. You struggle because of imperfections in your life—in your family relationships, or your work. You may struggle because of people who have hurt you deeply and you're having a hard time forgiving them. Or, perhaps you just don't feel close to God because of mistakes or sin in your life. You may be feeling inadequate or even believe yourself to be a failure as a Christian. So you lose the spiritual passion you had as a new believer, and continue onward in a survival mode, trying to make the best of whatever spiritual life you do have.

Becoming a Woman of Spiritual Passion

No matter what our circumstances or our level of spiritual growth, we all can be women of spiritual passion. This book will show you not only how to become more passionate in your Christian walk and your relationship with Jesus, but also how to have a spiritual passion that is absolutely contagious—a passion that others can't help but notice and want for themselves. Together, we will explore what spiritual passion is all about:

- becoming more aware of those things that can thwart your passion
- cultivating a deeper and more unshakeable faith

- developing a love for the things of God that cares little about what the world thinks

- embracing the perpetual joy given to you by Christ

- coming into God's presence and experiencing peace in the midst of difficult circumstances

- forgetting the things which are behind you and reaching forward to what lies ahead

- cultivating a spirit of praise and loving God with pure devotion

- being in constant amazement at God's Word—His love letter written to you

- making boldness a daily habit—this can be even for the shyest of women

- living in the Spirit that we might bear fruit for the Eternal City

- gaining victory over spiritual battles

- revival of the soul, which does not mean spasmodic excitement, but continuous and upward growth of the spiritual life

Daily we are on a heavenward walk—a fast-moving walk that's bringing us closer and closer to eternity. I certainly don't want, during my short stay on earth, to exist as a nominal Christian. How about you? So together, let's find and remove whatever thorns hinder our spiritual walk. It may hurt as we pull on those thorns, but we'll be walking much better after we've pulled them out. As a result, we'll have a more vigorous walk, a more ardent love, and a soul that thirsts after the things of God. And the loveliest part of all is that your life will become one that has *much to give.*

Ready for a spiritual boost? So am I.

PART 1:

Your Beloved's Promises

1

The Promise of a Better Future

*"I will restore you to health
and I will heal you of your wounds."*
—JEREMIAH 30:17

❧

A family tree that includes prestigious ancestors is usually a source of pride to that family. For example, the Keith clan in Scotland can be proud about some of their ancestors, who became leaders of Scotland's cavalry, fighting victoriously in just about every major battle over the centuries. Some of the men in the Keith family distinguished themselves in other ways: There was Sir Robert Keith, who signed Scotland's Declaration of Independence; George Keith, founder of Scotland's Marischal College (1593), and there was preacher James Keith, who left Scotland to preach Christ in Bridgewater, Massachusetts. He became well known in 1676 after saving the lives of the wife and child of Indian chief King Philip.[1]

But, just like any other family, the Keith clan had its fair share of black sheep. There were some members in the Keith clan who had serious sin issues—issues that ran deep and affected another clan, the Gunn clan. Between these two families were resentments, retaliations, and scores to be settled. So deep did their wounds go that their grudges lasted for 608 years, from 1370 to 1978.

It all started when Reginald Cheyne, a wealthy landowner, had a daughter named Mary. In 1370, Mary married John Keith. This meant that, by marriage, John Keith became the owner of a vast amount of land in the city of Caithness. This infuriated the Gunn clan, who themselves owned a lot of land in Caithness and didn't think that John Keith had any right to that land. Most likely, they privately resented the good fortune of John Keith, who didn't have to work hard, as they had, to get the land. The animosity that the Gunns felt toward John Keith was just the beginning of their enmity against all the Keiths.

In the early 1400s, Lachlan Gunn, a small proprietor in Braemore, had an only daughter named Helen, who was known as "the Beauty of Braemore." She was engaged to her cousin Alexander Gunn, whom she had known since childhood, and the wedding date was set.

One day Dugald Keith, who at the time was investing in his property, was passing through Braemore and saw Helen. He "made a dishonourable proposal which was indignantly rejected."[2] Dugald decided to achieve his end by force, and on the eve of Helen's wedding to Alexander, Dugald gathered quite a number of the Keith clan to go out and get Helen.

The Gunns were completely unprepared and taken by surprise when the Keiths arrived. Sadly, slaughter occurred on both sides. In the end the Gunns were defeated, and Helen was kidnapped and taken back to the Ackergill Tower, where Dugald Keith lived.

Because Helen couldn't escape the tower, she became determined to end her life. Not letting anyone in on her plan to commit suicide, Helen asked the keeper of Dugald's fortress if she might see the country from the top of the tower. He granted her request, and when he left the room, Helen threw herself headlong out the window. This grieved the Gunn family, who remembered this sad incident for years to come. Also, during the fourteenth and fifteenth centuries, the Gunns gradually lost all their land in the fertile parts of Caithness to the Keiths and to other clans who obtained grants of that land from the Scottish kings who were anxious to increase their influence over the fringes of their kingdom.

In 1478 (some say 1464), George Gunn of Crowner decided it was time to end the hate between the two clans. George sent communication to the Keiths that he wanted to initiate reconciliation and for them to meet at St. Tayre's Chapel, near the Ackergill Tower, where Helen had jumped to her death. The Keiths agreed to meet. But, upon their arrival they killed George, preferring to keep the fuel of hatred burning within their hearts.

Love and peace between the families finally came hundreds of years later, in 1978, when the Earl of Kintore (chief of the Keith clan) and Iain Gunn (the commander of the Gunn clan) signed a treaty of friendship between the two clans. They met at St. Tayre's Chapel, bringing an end to the 608-year-old feud.[3]

That's a long time to remain enemies! It was writer Horace Walpole (1717–1797) who said, "Life is a comedy to those who think, a tragedy to those who feel." The Gunn and Keith clans obviously *felt* very deeply about what had happened between them—so deeply, they couldn't let go of their hatred toward one another. This led to centuries of bitterness and unforgiveness. Imagine what could have happened if their passion had been expressed in positive ways rather than negative!

This brings up an important point: For as long as we nurse feelings of bitterness or hurt, we are unable to nurture a positive passion at any time. Both cannot co-exist in our hearts. How can we be passionate for spiritual things when our passion is focused on our hurts?

The Difficulty of Hurts

If we cling to our hurt in our heart and mind, there comes a chilling coldness within our soul; our spiritual life and the zeal that normally accompanies it becomes dull and somewhat lifeless. As well, our days are not filled with happiness or joy. Rather, our hurts or anger preoccupy us and spill over into other areas of our lives. For example, recently I received a call from a woman who had been asked to be a bridesmaid in a wedding. With great anxiety in her voice, she said, "Last night at the wedding rehearsal, the bride started yelling at some of her family members, recalling all the pain they had caused her years earlier. She even uninvited one of the bridesmaids from being in the wedding." The woman then said, "Donna, I don't want to be in this wedding! How can I get out of it?"

Sadly, that bride's anger was surfacing during a time that should have given her great joy. I recommended for the bridesmaid to "hang in there," and told her that although we cannot resolve the bride's feelings in an evening, we can encourage her with the following verse: "Look.... Observe! Be astonished! Wonder! Because *I am* doing something in your days—you would not believe if you were told" (Habakkuk 1:5). The bride needed to look at the wonderful things that the Lord was *currently* doing in her life, rather than look at her past hurts. This is a good lesson for us all—to look at the good things the Lord is doing in our lives. Among the great things He can do for us is to heal our wounds. This is His desire. He doesn't want us to look back, but rather ahead (Philippians 3:13-14)—ahead to a bright tomorrow and even a better future that's built upon rest and peace, happiness and joy. But His healing power doesn't come to just any of us. We must want it. We must ask for it. We're reminded, "You do not have because you do not ask" (James 4:2).

As women, we are social beings, and friends and family mean everything to us. So when we are hurt by those near to us, it's very easy for us to allow that hurt to affect us deeply. We'll find ourselves dwelling upon the causes for the hurt, upon the words that were said about us, upon the rejection we feel.

Physical pain seems at times to be easier to take than emotional pain. That's because the sting of emotional pain can linger in our inner being long after it was inflicted, whereas physical pain fades away after it's no longer applied.

While there are a variety of emotional wounds we could address (such as the wounds of divorce, wounds from physical abuse), we'll focus upon one major wound that puts all other emotional wounds into the same category. We'll look at the wounds we receive from the words of another, from the *cruelty of another person's tongue.* Almost all wounds involve some type of damaging communication. And one of the most common forms of this is slander, or gossip. A slanderer/gossiper carries injurious information from house to house, from heart to heart, and this information usually puts the victim in a negative light and can go so far as to ruin the victim's reputation. While a murderer kills the body, a gossiper or slanderer kills the character.

The Instigator of Hurts

Years ago, while attempting to finish a manuscript on Mormonism (shortly due to the publisher), I received a most unexpected phone call. It was from an irate woman who communicated some very cruel, vicious, and attacking words. They were words to kill the spirit (Proverbs 14:4), words like a sword "sharpened to make a slaughter, polished to flash like lightning!" (Ezekiel 21:10). Completely caught off guard, I *tried* to explain to her that her attack was based on a misunderstanding. But she never let me explain that. Instead, she sharply slammed the phone down and then called the next person on her list to talk about me.

After that woman hung up, a most horrendous and overpowering thought entered my mind. It was the evil one saying, "Your reputation is now ruined, you might as well 'end it all' this very minute."

I love life, and so the thought of killing myself had *never, ever* entered into my mind until that very second. Really, there are no words that can adequately express how horrible that moment was, of having pressed upon my mind the mere thought of ending my life. I knew this was from the enemy, so I immediately went to the Word of God, which eliminated that dark and evil thought. The Word also helped me, during subsequent days, when some people left messages on my answering machines wanting to talk about what they were hearing. It was during this time I had to stay focused. For had I allowed it, those calls could have taken up much of my time and emotional energy. Surely the enemy was trying to get my mind off what the Lord wanted me to accomplish, such as finish a manuscript that would help Christian women reach Mormon women for Christ. He also wanted to cause me to be an ineffective and depressed Christian—not to mention an angry Christian. He didn't want me to be spiritually passionate for Jesus and His kingdom.

The devil, whose name means "slanderer," often wounds through slander not only because he's living up to his name, but because slander can spread so quickly. I saw this clearly when, about a month after that terrible phone call, I was in the post office and had to give some information to the clerk. When I gave my name, a woman standing next to me said, "Your name sounds so familiar." She then gave me the name of her church and asked if I went there. I responded, "No, I don't attend your church, but I know the Lord is doing great things there."

She then asked, "Do you know some of my friends?" She then mentioned some people whom I might know.

I replied, "No, I'm sorry I don't know any of them."

She then said, "This is really bugging me! I know your name from somewhere!"

I finally volunteered, "Perhaps you've read one of my books?"

She thought for a moment and exclaimed, "Oh, now I know! You're that woman who...." She then interrupted herself and, trying to be as delicate and diplomatic as possible, began to share with me what she had heard about me. She spoke kindly, but what she had heard about me was clearly erroneous. I couldn't help but wonder how many people had passed along this information about me before it got to her. How true it is, "rumor will be added to rumor" (Ezekiel 7:26).

It's a given. As you and I live passionately for God, we will be attacked, and often through slander. The devil slandered God to Eve (Genesis 3:1,4-5), and slandered Job to God (Job 1:11; 2:4). He slandered Paul (Acts 13:45,50; 17:13; 18:12-13) and Jesus (Luke 5:21) by using the mouths of others. He uses the mouths of both nonbelievers and Christians who are, at the time, walking in the flesh rather than in the Spirit. Certainly, the attacking words of a fellow believer are the most painful, and bring the deepest wound.

Satan has even used powerful ministers against one another. George Whitefield (1714–1770) was a pastor and missionary who pointed many people to God during the 1700s, and John Wesley was a Methodist pastor who did the same. Wesley and Whitefield, during their early years, were both part of a Methodist group called "The Holy Club" (a club that based salvation upon good works, contrary to what Scripture teaches in Ephesians 2:8-9). During this time, Whitefield became born again. Appalled, John Wesley (prior to himself becoming born-again[4]) became vehement in his criticism against Whitefield[5] and tried to ruin his new ministry as an evangelical pastor, calling him "a fiend from hell."[6]

Perhaps you have a friend, a loved one, or a fellow believer who has spoken viciously against you. It hurts, doesn't it? But we can't let slander or verbal attacks get us down. We've got to keep in mind that Satan is behind such conduct, and that we are in the midst of a spiritual battle. Satan only bothers those who are making an impact *for* God's kingdom and thus are working *against* his kingdom. And after Satan wounds you, he will do whatever he can to keep you down. How?

First, by bringing to your mind, over and over again, the horrible words spoken against you. The enemy wants you to believe that *you have the right* to be upset about the harm done to you. All this does is stir up anger in your heart. Though you may initially be right when you say, "Yes, injustice was done to me," the original complaint is often lost because of what we are creating in the heart—selfish resentments, ill feelings, and bitterness. Such attitudes are rebuked in Scripture: "Is this the love you show your friend?" (2 Samuel 16:17 NIV). If hostility, resentment, and anger take possession of us, we will end up creating our own injustices and wrongs toward the one who hurt us. This is what Satan wants. He will do whatever he can to get your eyes off Jesus and onto your accuser and the cruel words she spoke. And, if he can get you to desire revenge, all the better.

Next, Satan tries to get you to *believe* what your attacker said about you. He wants you to think you're no good...you amount to nothing... you have nothing to offer to others. By getting you to accept his lies, he can diminish your passion for Christ and your effectiveness as a Christian.

But what are you going to believe—what God says about you, or what your accuser says? It's impossible to believe both ways. For instance, let's say that because of someone's misunderstanding or misjudgments, you have been accused of being a liar. But you know that before God, your conscience is clear. So, if your accuser has called you a liar, but you have been a proclaimer of truth, then what is really true about you? Don't allow a false accusation to fester in your mind and cause you to stumble. Turn your eyes away from your attacker and onto God. The enemy will try very hard to zap your zeal, to keep you down, to crush your heart, and to shut God out of your world.

When the actions and words of another are cruel toward us, they frequently affect our thought life. We are tempted to let them eat away at our heart, our soul, and our mind. Sometimes our hurt is so overwhelming that we cannot sleep at night.

Our comfort is that we are not alone in this. For example, take a look at David, who, because of his adversaries, said, "I am weary with my sighing; every night I make my bed swim, I dissolve my couch with my tears" (Psalm 6:5). Another psalmist in distress said, "My tears have been my food day and night, while they say to me all day long, 'Where is your God?'" (Psalm 42:3). Asaph exclaimed, "In the day of my trouble I sought the Lord, in the night my hand was stretched out....I am so troubled that I cannot speak" (Psalm 77:2,4).

Have you felt troubled like David and Asaph? Have you felt defeated and all alone because of cruel slander or gossip? When we are verbally attacked, it's so easy for our mind to revisit that painful scene, going over those vicious words again and again, as if the accuser were throwing them at us afresh.

When we are slandered, we must not dwell upon the dark, depressing thoughts that may enter our mind. How healthy is that? How does it help our soul? How does it change things? How does it assist us in being more productive the following day? Most of all, how does it help us have a zealous passion for Jesus? When we have sleepless nights, we need to go to the Lord for help. He, of all who ever lived on earth, knows how we feel! He, too, had verbal attacks against Him. Though Jesus exhibited a perfect, gentle, loving character, the foul imaginations of men ascribed the evil attributes of Satan to Jesus (Luke 11:15-18).

The Response to Our Hurts

Going to the Lord Through S.L.E.E.P.

The pastor of the early church in Antioch, John Chrysostom (A.D. 347–407), said, "No man is ever really hurt by anyone but himself." He's right. As long as we allow other people's hurtful words to control our thoughts, we can hurt ourselves physically (ulcers, nervous tension, and other ailments) or spiritually (through an angry or even bitter spirit). To keep from hurting ourselves, and from having sleepless nights, we need S.L.E.E.P. We need to...

S tay in God's Word

L eave everything in His hands

E arnestly meditate upon Him

E mbrace His comfort, and

P ray

In this way, we will receive powerful healing from God.

1. *Stay in God's Word.* Our Bridegroom, Jesus, tells us, "My words... are life unto those that find them, and health to all their flesh" (Proverbs 4:20,22 KJV). At night, before you turn off the light, grab your Bible (keep it next to your bed) and read divine words of healing, such as, "The LORD is good, a stronghold in the day of trouble, and He knows those who take refuge in Him" (Nahum 1:7); "You are my hiding place; You preserve me from trouble; You surround me with songs of deliverance" (Psalm 32:7); and "Those who sow in tears shall reap with joyful shouting" (Psalm 126:5). (For more promises, refer to endnote 7 on page 233).

2. *Leave everything in God's hands.* I love it when my husband, Brian, says to me, "Just leave everything to me; I'll take care of it." There's comfort in having someone else handle a burden. But Brian can't take care of everything. While he's a wonderful husband and spiritual leader, he can't change people's hearts—my heart, or that of an accuser. Only our Heavenly Groom can do that—and it's He who tells us that if we cast our burdens upon Him, He will sustain us and never allow us to be shaken (Psalm 55:22). This is what King David did. He could have become very bitter against his enemies. He could have used revenge. He could have been outright mean. Instead, he went right to the Lord, asking that *He* take care of them: "Do not let those who are wrongfully my enemies rejoice over me; nor let those who hate me without cause wink maliciously" (Psalm 35:19). David knew he could trust the Supernatural One, the Ultimate One who confronts injustice: "What do you mean by crushing My people and grinding the face of the poor?" (Isaiah 3:15).

Remember John Wesley's critical comment about George Whitefield? Later, Wesley, as a true believer, came to understand Whitefield and the lonely struggles he faced. At Whitefield's funeral, Wesley proclaimed:

> Not only was his reputation lost, and some of his dearest
> friends forsook him, but he was exercised with inward

trials, and those of the severest kind. Many nights he lay sleepless upon his bed; many days, prostrate on the ground. But after he had groaned several months under "the spirit of bondage," God was pleased to remove the heavy load.[8]

Whether it be John Whitefield over 200 years ago or us today, we must leave our concerns about our character and our accuser in God's hands so that He can remove our heavy load. He knows the truth of the matter, and that's all that counts (Romans 8:31). Really, we can well afford the unfriendliness of others if we have the approval of Jesus. Consider Mary, who anointed Jesus with costly perfume. Judas was quite critical of her (John 12:4), but she had no need to fear what he thought—especially after Jesus said, "Let her alone" (John 12:7). We must simply trust God with the outcome. And, in light of the bliss we will know in eternity, the harm done to us today is a drop in the bucket.

3. *Earnestly meditate upon God.* When we turn off the light at night, rather than dwelling on our hurtful situation, we can do what other godly people have done—think about God. "When I remember You on my bed, I meditate on You in the night watches" (Psalm 63:6). "At night my soul longs for You, indeed, my spirit within me seeks You diligently" (Isaiah 26:9). As we meditate, we can think about the fact that our Beloved says, "I have called you by name; you are Mine!" (Isaiah 43:1). We can be thrilled that we belong to Jesus. We can think about His love, protection, guidance, blessings, spiritual healing through salvation (Isaiah 54:4; John 14:6), and so much more (see endnote 9 on page 233 for assistance).

4. *Embrace God's comfort.* British preacher Frederick W. Robertson (1816–1853) said, "The mistake we make is to look for a source of comfort in ourselves: self-contemplation, instead of gazing upon God. In other words, we look for comfort precisely where comfort never can be."[10]

Robertson was so right! Only Jesus can help us, for He is the God of *all* comfort and consolation (2 Corinthians 1:3; 7:6). His comfort is like a husband's love (Hosea 2:14)—a husband who tells his bride, in dear, loving words, "Do not let your heart be troubled" (John 14:1).

If we choose not to receive God's comfort, we'll not only remain in our gloom, we'll also begin to think wrongly of Him. This is what happened to Asaph. He refused to be comforted (Palm 77:2), and began to think God had rejected him, forgotten to be gracious toward him, and was angry with him rather than compassionate toward him (Psalm 77:7-9). How clearly we need divine comfort, a comfort that heals us of our wounds and receives encouragement in Christ, consolation of love, and fellowship of the Spirit along with affection and compassion (Philippians 2:1).

5. *Pray.* I know that if I never communicated with Brian, he would not only feel hurt, but we certainly wouldn't have much of a marriage. Throughout the Old Testament, we can see how God felt hurt when the Israelites not only stopped communicating with Him, but forgot about Him: "Can a virgin forget her ornaments, or a bride her attire? Yet My people have forgotten Me days without number" (Jeremiah 2:32). As the bride of Christ, let's make sure we don't forget our Bridegroom, especially when it comes to communicating with Him. As you lay in your bed, talk to the Lord rather than dwell upon your hurt. Ask Him to help you not only meditate upon Him, but guide *all* your thoughts toward those things that are true, honorable, right, pure, lovely, of good repute, excellent, and worthy of praise (Philippians 4:8). Prayer works! He *will* help you (Psalm 6:8-9).

> *As* the bride of Christ, let's make sure we don't forget our Bridegroom, especially when it comes to communicating with Him.

Following these five steps will assist us greatly in healing our wounds because they draw us closer to Jesus. But there's one remaining step we must take if we want complete healing and to be near to Jesus. For some of us, it's not an easy step to take. But it must be done—we must *forgive*.

Granting Forgiveness

When we have an unforgiving spirit, we can't move on in our spiritual life. We can't be both bitter in our heart and passionate about our Lord Jesus, about the things He has called us to accomplish, about growing in our spiritual life. It's not that we don't want to be passionate about these things—*because we do!* But an unforgiving spirit hinders our spiritual progress.

Jesus, who knew the damage that can be done to our spiritual life when we harbor unforgiveness, says, "Forgive" (Mark 11:25). Forgive, not up to seven times, as Peter suggested (Matthew 18:21), but rather "up to seventy times seven" (Matthew 18:22). In other words, we are to forgive indefinitely.

God's mercy is boundless, so must ours be. Like the slave who was indebted to the king (Matthew 18:25-26), so are we indebted to God. We can't pay back what we owe. He gave us everything and forgave us of everything. He provided us His grace so that no root of bitterness would ever spring up from our heart. Bitterness causes nothing but trouble and defiles many (Hebrews 12:15). Are we resting in the grace of Jesus? If not, we can't help but be bitter; we can't help but defile others (such as family members). Most of all, we can't help but defile ourselves. We become like the unmerciful slave who thought mercy was a good thing when it was given to him, yet refused to show similar mercy to another. Because of this, he was called "wicked" (Matthew 18:32). May that never be said of us!

As women of spiritual passion, we are called to live out the example of Christ. We are told that Jesus "suffered *for you*, leaving you an example for you to follow in His steps" (1 Peter 2:21). The example we are to follow is to make sure that we ourselves aren't committing a sin (1 Peter 2:22), that we aren't retaliating and hurting others in the same manner that they hurt us (1 Peter 2:23). We're to forgive those who hurt us, "just as the Lord forgave" us (Colossians 3:13). Jesus forgave those who tortured Him and put Him on a cross (Luke 23:34). If we say we're followers of Jesus, shouldn't we do no less? Without forgiveness we'll never heal; we can have no divine forgiveness for ourselves (Matthew 6:12; Mark 11:25). Nor can we have love. How is it that we can cling to Jesus and, at the same time, have unforgiveness in our hearts? We can't.

We are also to pray for those who hurt us. Jesus said, "I say to you, love your enemies and pray for those who persecute you.... For if you love those who love you, what reward do you have?" (Matthew 5:44,46). Jesus is showing us that in life, we must accept not only the good, but the bad; not only love to man, but the struggle to keep that love. And, it can be a struggle: "In return for my love they act as my accusers; *but I am in prayer*" (Psalm 109:4). We must pray to have a love that is patient under injustice, to have a love for those cruel toward us, and to have a love that feels sorry for those who hurt us.

Yes, we should also feel sorry for the person who hurt us. Now, expressing sympathy for an enemy does not amount to tolerating her sin. You can still love a person without agreeing with her words or actions. And her sin *will* bear consequences, because not one of us can sin with impunity. Every sin carries its penalty. It may be that God will allow her to experience the very pain that she inflicted upon you: "As you have done, it will be done to you. Your dealings will return on your own head" (Obadiah 15). This same idea is repeated by Christ: "By your standard of measure, it will be measured to you" (Matthew 7:2).

Remember when Jacob deceived his father in regard to Esau (Genesis 27:1-46)? Well, he in turn would be deceived by his own sons in regard to Joseph (Genesis 37:31-34). Remember when Laban deceived Jacob

(Genesis 29:15-30)? In turn, Jacob, from Laban's point of view, deceived him (Genesis 31:26-29).

The deceiver herself is deceived, the dishonest is cheated, the hater is hated, and the cruel person is often ruthlessly treated. Imagine the pain those who hurt us eventually receive—it's the very judgment of God. I certainly wouldn't want such pain. Nor do we want it for those who hurt us, *unless* it's designed to bring them to repentance. But still, we want our heart to stay tender toward *all* who are hurting—even our enemies. Just as Jesus loved His enemies while He hung on the cross, He tells us, "love your enemies" (Matthew 5:44).

How can we best love? By responding with love to those who hurt us: "Do good to those who hate you, bless those who curse you, pray for those who mistreat you" (Luke 6:27-28). We can also be concerned for the salvation of our enemies (if they aren't saved), and pray that ultimately, in the end, their lives will have changed, to the glory of God.

> Dear Lord,
>
> Please be with those who have caused me pain.
> Help me to forgive, while You take away their shame.
> Bring them into Calvary's fold,
> And for eternity, together, we'll speak of Your mercies,
>   untold.
>
> —D.M.

The Questions about Hurts and Forgiveness

I once had a lengthy conversation with a woman who was struggling with the whole matter of forgiveness. She asked, "What if the person who hurt me doesn't ask for forgiveness?" In such a case, should we still forgive? I responded, "Forgive for your own sake." Forgiveness has a way of helping us eliminate our grief. And we need to forgive for the offender's sake. Jesus will work out everything—the hurt, the pain, the entire incident—for not only our good, but hers also, if she is a believer (Romans 8:28).

The woman also asked, "Must I return to the damaged friendship as if nothing happened? And, if I don't return to it, will that be a sign of bitterness on my part?" Answering such questions is difficult because only God knows the true intent in the hearts of the offender and the victim. But first, we know that the Lord *can* repair broken relationships. "Is anything too difficult for the LORD?" (Genesis 18:14). But we must also realize there may be times when the Lord might not want us going back into the relationship. He warns that "the companion of fools will suffer harm" (Proverbs 13:20 and more[11]), and not to associate with a person given to anger (Proverbs 22:24). So to stay away from a relationship, by the Lord's admonition, does not show we are bitter, but rather obedient.

In reality, for any relationship to become healthy again, *both parties* would have to turn to the Lord. It takes two people to make a bargain, just as it takes two people to reconcile. It's my own personal opinion that the first step toward repairing that relationship should come from the *injured one*. Why? It's possible the person who harmed you doesn't know you've been injured. We should do whatever we can and "try to conciliate" (1 Corinthians 4:13). If that doesn't work, we should simply forgive and not force ourselves on someone who doesn't want to repair the relationship.

Ultimately, the bottom line is, if harm has come to a relationship, no matter whether or not it can be repaired, it's up to us to have a forgiving spirit and "pursue peace with all men" (Hebrews 12:14). But we can't do it without Jesus' help. He was zealous in love—and He loved to the end (Luke 23:43, John 19:26-27). He was zealous in forgiveness, and He forgave to the end (Luke 23:34). He was zealous in making peace with *all* men—and He was peaceable to the end (Matthew 26:50-56).

Most of all, He was zealous in sharing His concerns with the Father, because "I and the Father are one" (John 10:30).

The Promise to Those Who Hurt

Living out this same zeal of love, of forgiveness, of peace, and of giving the Lord all our concerns, including our wounds, we will most assuredly receive the promise, "I will restore you to health and I will heal you of your wounds" (Jeremiah 30:17). What a promise for a better future! Rather than face the days ahead with your hurts and pains, you face them as a healed woman—ever growing, becoming more like Jesus, becoming more and more attractive to Him like *a bride adorned for her husband.*[12] Not one of us can look more beautiful than this!

Our Passion in Action

1. Are you struggling over a problem now? Write in a journal your steps to S.L.E.E.P. For instance, what scriptures have helped you while staying in the Word? What matters are you submitting to the Lord's hands? What are your thoughts of God as you earnestly think upon Him? What do you appreciate most about God's comfort? Finish with a prayer to God about your struggle.

2. Is there someone, whether in the past or present, who has hurt you? Have you forgiven that person? If not, what steps might you need to take to help you through the process of forgiveness?

3. Is there someone you have *already* forgiven? How has that forgiveness rejuvenated your soul? What are three or four benefits of forgiving and moving on?

4. Think about the last time you were wounded by the words or actions of another. Why do you think you were attacked? What were you doing, or what were you involved in, at the time you were attacked?

5. When you've been attacked spiritually, where do you need to turn your focus, and why?

2

The Promise of Protection and Strength

"Do not fear, for I am with you;
do not be dismayed, for I am your God.
I will strengthen you and help you;
I will uphold you with my righteous right hand."
—ISAIAH 41:10 NIV

When Sarah Pardee was born in September 1839 in New Haven, Connecticut, her parents Leonard and Sarah were obviously joyous. Yet little did they know that this precious baby would one day live her life in such fear that it would paralyze her from life itself. But during her early years, there was no need for concern. Sarah became an accomplished pianist, fluent in various languages, and was the charm and attraction of many men in New Haven, including one man in particular, William Winchester.

William was the son of Oliver Winchester, who invented the Volcanic Repeater, the rifle used by the Union soldiers all through the Civil War. The Winchesters became very wealthy from not only government contracts during the war, but from public sales. It wasn't long before William proposed to Sarah, she accepted, and they had an elaborate ceremony that knew no budget. Shortly after the wedding, William took over his father's rifle company. His greatest pride was making vast improvements on the Volcanic Repeater, which he renamed the Winchester Rifle.

Four years into the Winchester's marriage, Sarah gave birth to a daughter, Annie Pardee Winchester. Sadly, Annie lived only nine days. She was diagnosed with a childhood disease known as maramus, which deprives the body of protein and causes the body to lose weight. In essence, she started dying from the very moment she took her first breath. This tragic loss caused Sarah to go into a deep depression for the next ten years. When she came out of her depression, she began to enjoy life again—but that enjoyment was short-lived. Five years later, William died of pulmonary tuberculosis.

Becoming the sole heir of the Winchester fortune and one of the wealthiest woman in the world meant nothing to Sarah, who had lost what meant most to her. Sadly, it was during this time that she began to live in a world of fear—fear primarily caused by a spiritist medium whom Sarah had sought for counsel. She was told by the spiritist that the spirits of thousands upon thousands of people who died by the Winchester Rifle were seeking vengeance. They had gotten some satisfaction from taking Sarah's daughter and husband, but now they wanted to take Sarah. The medium told Sarah that the only way for her to stay alive was to build a home for herself and the spirits, giving each of them a room. She was told to continue building all the remaining days of her life. The moment she stopped building rooms would supposedly be the moment she would die.

Panic and fear absorbed Sarah's thoughts and actions. In 1884, she moved to California's Santa Clara Valley and started building on 162 acres of land. She hired 22 carpenters and assigned them to morning and evening shifts. They hammered and sawed 24 hours a day, never stopping even for a moment.

Sarah was so greatly distressed that she believed the 1906 San Francisco earthquake was her fault because she was almost finished with the building of her home—something the spiritist told her never to do. She blocked off 30 rooms damaged by the quake with the idea this would keep the home from ever being complete, and would also block off, forever, some of the spirits she thought had occupied those rooms. Still, Sarah continued on with building more rooms. And in the midst of all this, she feared something else—the outside world. She was rarely ever seen in her carriage, fearing great harm would come to her if she roamed around town.

Thirty-six years later, on the morning of Sarah's death, the hammering and sawing finally stopped. By this time, approximately 160 rooms had been built and completely furnished, as well as three elevators and 47 fireplaces (most of which had no purpose). There is a chimney that rises four floors and stops short of the ceiling. Several closets open to a steep drop to the outdoor lawn below. Some doors open into blank walls. Many of the bathrooms have glass doors on them. One room has a window built into the floor, and another has a door in the floor. There are various staircases that lead to nowhere, and one staircase that leads to the ceiling. All the staircases have 13 steps, except for one that has 42 steps. Normally 42 steps would span three stories, but not in this house. This staircase was only nine feet tall because each step is two inches high. As far as the stair posts, all were installed upside-down. These are just a few of the many eccentricities in the home[1] that Sarah built—all designed to trample down the spirits, to fool and confuse them. Sarah believed these bizarre features would help protect her.

If only Sarah had never made her appointment with the spiritist, but instead had turned to God, who is "near to the brokenhearted, and saves those who are crushed in spirit" (Psalm 34:18). He promises, "I will instruct you and teach you in the way which you should go; I will counsel you with My eye upon you" (Psalm 32:8). Just imagine how different Sarah's life would have been here on earth and into eternity!

Thankfully, we who have chosen to seek the Lord's counsel and protection will never find ourselves in Sarah's shoes. However, we do share a common enemy—Satan. He goes about as a roaring lion, seeking whom he may devour. Because we are the bride of Jesus, we are his greatest target. Though he can't have us (Hebrews 13:5), if we allow, he can make a mess of us. And there are several kinds of fear he uses.

In the last chapter, we saw that one way the enemy attempts to blow out our spiritual passion is through the attacks of others. Now we're going to look at a different tactic he uses—fear from within. Through fear, he can paralyze our thinking and blind us from common sense. His goal is to crush and deaden our spiritual life. He knows that fear can sap the spiritual energy out of us. And there are several kinds of fear he uses.

Fears That Plague Us

Fears for Our Loved Ones

One day while waiting in a long line at the grocery store, I overheard two women in conversation. The first said, "Whenever the phone rings before 8:00 AM, I think it's a call to tell me that my mother is dead."

The second woman asked, "Is your mother in poor health?"

The first replied, "No, she's fine, but I fear so much her death that I just assume the call is going to be bad news about my mother."

Through the years I've talked to other women with similar fears about their loved ones. Fear of a husband or child dying despite their good health. Fear of a husband leaving for another woman despite a wonderful marriage. Fear of a child being kidnapped despite all safety precautions. And a host of personal fears as well.

Personal Fears

We all have fears—such as the fear of pain, of getting cancer, of dying. There are some who fear leaving the house (believing something awful could happen), going to church (because of hurt from other church-goers), never getting married, being home alone at night, and mysterious sounds of the night.

Past experiences can result in present fears. For instance, I know a Christian woman whose husband had an adulterous affair and eventually left her. She hesitates to remarry, fearing it could happen to her again.

Fears That Warp Our Perception

Just the other day a Christian woman told me she has a genuine fear of birds. Not wanting to sound disrespectful, but coming across a bit surprised, I asked, "How could you have a fear of birds?" She said, "Ever since I saw the Hitchcock movie *The Birds,* those critters have terrified me."

Our fears may not be as unusual as that, but generally, our fears can become so vivid that they warp our perception of reality. For example, I once had a fear of flying. Over 20 years ago, coming home from a missions trip to Costa Rica and Honduras, I was aboard a plane that came very close to crashing into the Caribbean Sea. With the plane out of control, people were falling out of their seats, some were vomiting, and many were crying and screaming in Spanish, "*¡Nos vamos a morir! ¡Nos vamos a morir!*"[2] Others were exclaiming the same cry in English: "We're going to die! We're going to die!" While I wasn't panicky like the others, I was in shock. I began to wonder, *Will they find me in one piece, or several?* I then surmised I'd probably never be found at all.

Fortunately, we didn't crash. We made an emergency landing in British Honduras (now known as Belize). Despite the tremendous witnessing opportunities that arose with one woman, after that episode I couldn't even *think* about boarding an airplane again. I was afraid I might go through the same horrible experience again.

Obviously, my perception was warped and didn't match reality. When you consider the many hundreds of thousands of flights all over the world every year that occur without incident, you know the chances of a repeat experience are incredibly small. As comforting as it is to understand that the probabilities were vastly in my favor, they alone weren't enough for me to overcome my fear of flying.

Truly, many of our fears are based on imagined scenarios that almost never come to fruition. How easily we can find ourselves fretful over things to the point that fear controls us, takes over our lives, and dictates what we do and don't do, where we go or don't go, who we talk to or avoid. We possess fears of circumstances that have almost no chance of materializing, and as a result, we become paralyzed from taking positive action and moving forward in life.

Fear of Man

Some of us are intimidated by those who seem to have greater talent, intellectual power, wealth, rank, and social influence than we do. We fear what they think about us or their rejection. Worse yet, we may fear what an evil person might do to us—such as harm our reputation, our property, or our physical well-being. The fear of man is one of the most common fears that can affect our faith. We might think, *How can I ever overcome that?* Scripture assures us by saying, "The Lord is my helper, I will not be afraid. What will man do to me?" (Hebrews 13:6). To really believe this powerful verse, we need to stand firm in our faith—it's the only way. Let me explain.

Long ago, while a college student, I had a boss whom we'll call Mr. Smitty. He made me very nervous. He had a terrible temper, never smiled, and seemed determined to make everyone's day miserable. What I didn't like most about him was that he wanted me, on occasion, to lie for him. Each and every time he approached me with a new way of deceiving one of his potential clients, I just wouldn't take part. Such deceit, for him, meant an opportunity to make quite a bit of money. For obvious reasons, his greedy mind wanted me to obey him. I frequently thought about leaving and looking for a new job, but I knew that my boss and others needed Jesus, so I felt at that time a responsibility to stay.

One day a gentleman called the office and asked for Mr. Smitty. My boss, knowing who was on hold for him, approached me and told me to take the call. He told me to give the client some information that I knew was false. I said, "I can't lie to that man."

Mr. Smitty ignored my comment and, in a threatening tone, said, "You better get on that phone and tell him what I told you. I'll be on the other extension listening to every word you say."

Just before I picked up the phone I quickly prayed, "Dear Jesus, help me!"

I began by responding to the potential client's inquiries. I could see my boss in the other room, with the phone to his ear, pacing back and forth. Ignoring what I saw by sight, *I had to trust in what I couldn't see*—what the Lord would do in this situation. As I continued to talk, I gave the gentleman all the facts I knew to be true. I explained these facts in such a way that would make it difficult for my boss to lie to this man at a later time. When I got off the phone, my boss approached my desk with a deep-red face. His eyeballs looked as if they were going to pop out. Thrusting his finger at me repeatedly, he yelled, "Lie! Lie! Lie! Lie! Lie! Lie! Lie!"

Sad, isn't it? Amazingly, I wasn't fired. As the Bible says, "Who is there to harm you if you prove zealous for what is good?" (2 Peter 3:13). While I may have proved zealous for what was good, let's imagine what would have happened had I not stood firm in my faith:

Had I not stood firm, I would have become morally weak, following the bad example of my boss because I feared losing my job or receiving his ridicule.

Had I not stood firm, I would have made it much harder, in the future, to try taking a stand for what was right.

Had I not stood firm, I would have compromised my convictions and would have endorsed the evil course my boss was taking.

Had I not stood firm, I would have disobeyed Jesus and betrayed Him—which my boss would have been only too happy to see.

Had I not stood firm, my witness and example to others at that office would have been completely destroyed.

When we do not stand firm, our fear wins and makes us out to be hypocrites. Instead of having a strong faith that refuses to bow to others, we let others have power over our faith—they weaken it, they control it. No wonder the fear of man is so often condemned in Scripture! (See, for example, Isaiah 51:7; Jeremiah 1:8; Ezekiel 2:6; 3:9; Matthew 10:26,28; Luke 12:4; 1 Peter 3:14.)

Scripture says, "If you do not stand firm in your faith, you will not stand at all" (Isaiah 7:9 NIV). When we are put in awkward situations, rather than fear people, we must fear God *and* believe Him. "For he who comes to God must believe that He is" (Hebrews 11:6).

Belief is *everything.* It has an impact on what we do. Let's look at it this way: If we *don't* believe that strawberries will grow in our garden, we won't plant them, right? Likewise, if we don't truly believe God's promise of strength and protection, we won't seek it. If we don't believe He will help us *in whatever* situation, we won't seek His help. Instead, we'll stay in our fear and discouragement. Only the spiritually passionate person stands firm in trust and confidence in God (Psalm 91:2). Without this faith, it's "impossible to please Him" (Hebrews 11:6).

> *J*esus, who has vowed to protect us, understands all the possible fears we could have.

Jesus, who has vowed to protect us, understands all the possible fears we could have. And, like any loving husband would say to his wife, Jesus says, "Do not be afraid" (Matthew 14:27). First Peter 3:6 speaks of doing "what is right without being frightened *by any fear."* Jesus, our role model, feared nothing. He didn't fear those who attacked or betrayed Him

(Matthew 13:53-58), He didn't fear the temptations that confronted Him (Matthew 4:1-11), nor did He fear Satan (Matthew 4:10). He didn't fear His enemies as they took Him to His death (Matthew 26:45-54). Yes, He is our true example of one who feared nothing. Can we be like Him and *fear nothing*?

Can We Fear Nothing?

When both of my children were toddlers, they *loved* a little book we had about the story of Jesus and the big storm (based on Matthew 8:23-27). They wanted me to read to the story to them every day. It wasn't long before they had memorized it and wanted to recite the story to me. One day I asked four-year-old Michelle, "Why do you like this story so much?" She didn't even have to think about her response. She quickly answered, "Because Jesus shows me I don't need to be afraid."

Michelle is right. Jesus does show us that. While in a storm so furious that waves were sweeping water into the boat, He never once showed fear. Rather, He slept. The disciples, however, were afraid and woke Jesus, saying, "We are perishing!" It was right that they went to the One who could help them, but they were wrong to be seized by fear. Jesus rebuked them, saying, "Why are you afraid, you men of little faith?"

Now, note that Jesus *didn't* first calm the storm and then rebuke them. No, while the wind and the sea was still tumultuous and on the verge of capsizing the boat, Jesus rebuked the disciples for their fear. Now, you and I might think this is a bit harsh. After all, didn't it seem they might drown? Why not be fearful?

I believe one of the reasons why Jesus rebuked the disciples was because, in the span of a day, they had already seen Jesus heal a man of leprosy (Matthew 8:1-4), heal a centurion's servant of paralysis (Matthew 8:5-13), and heal Peter's mother-in-law of a fever (Matthew 8:14-15). When evening came, Jesus gave "just a word" and healed "many who were demon-possessed" (Matthew 8:16-17). And a few days earlier, Jesus had told the disciples, "Do not be worried....who of you by being worried can add a *single* hour to his life?" (Matthew 6:25,27).

Might Jesus need to rebuke us? Have we not seen the ways the Lord has come through for us and others? Haven't we known His nearness? His help? He is observant and always present. He is never absent, nor ignorant of any circumstance in our life. So why are we anxious? "I am with you," He says (Isaiah 41:10). How often do we forget this truth?

Along with forgetting God's presence, we tend to forget that He has given us a purpose. If our purpose on earth has not yet been fulfilled, then regardless of our circumstances, our life *will not* end. When we think this way, we aren't so prone to panic. If the disciples had thought that way, they wouldn't have panicked either. Did they think that Jesus, their Master, would allow them all to drown that very moment? Was their purpose as disciples going to end before Jesus' ministry really got started? Were their voices going to be silenced before they had started proclaiming the kingdom's message?

We can indeed live *without* fear when we *firmly* believe Jesus is always with us and that He has a purpose for us to fulfill. Don't let fear cripple you. Fear will prevent you from exercising faith and will allow your circumstances to overwhelm you.

What Are We Communicating to Others?

There was a time when Martin Luther, a former Catholic priest and the courageous leader of the Reformation, fell into a state of depression, lethargy, and great sadness. No one knows exactly what circumstances led him to these feelings, although the loss of two of his children[3] may have been a factor. Unfortunately, it seemed nothing could bring him out of his despair. His wife, Katherine, tried to help, but nothing seemed to work. So she put on her black mourning dress, with a heavy black veil covering her face. She wore it all around the house.

Martin was concerned and asked her why she had done this. She replied, "God is dead." Martin dismissed Katherine's words as nonsense, and she responded that Martin's severe depression had shown her God is dead. "If He weren't" said Katherine, "you would use your great faith in Him to help you out of this lethargy." Luther saw that she was right, and he returned to his passionate faith in the Almighty.

Like Martin Luther, we can all wallow about in a sort of midnight gloom rather than allow the Lord's face to shine upon us (Numbers 6:25). We can find ourselves fretful and distrustful toward God, thinking He has forgotten about us. And when our fears and discouragements become transparent for all to see, they communicate, in essence, that God cannot help us, that He is dead, that He is no longer working in our lives. The cumulative result? Our spiritual passion is zapped. We are no longer excited about the things of the Lord, nor do we talk about Jesus as if He's the love of our life.

But no matter how terrible our circumstances, we *can* have trust and confidence in God. He's not dead, but alive (John 14:6), and He hasn't changed because He doesn't change (Malachi 3:6). If we think God has changed, it's actually us who have changed. We may feel we have lost the warmth of His love, but we will never lose His love itself. We may feel we have lost the comfort of His grace, but we will never lose His grace. We may feel we have lost the joy of our salvation, but we will never lose our salvation. Oh, let us not allow such discouragement in our lives! This type of despair, the very type the Lord says *not to have* (Isaiah 41:10), keeps us in fear and distrust. It also produces consequences and missed opportunities.

Consequences and Missed Opportunities

Usually when we succumb to fear, we have forgotten (like the disciples) past events that should have taught us there is no need to fear.

For instance, consider the Israelites. Despite their *knowing* that God would help them fight the Amorites; despite their having *seen with their own eyes* the Lord help them fight the Egyptians; and despite Moses telling them, "Do not be shocked, nor fear them," the Israelites still lived in fear and lacked trust in the Lord (Deuteronomy 1:27-32). The consequence? They were not allowed to enter the Promised Land (Deuteronomy 1:35). The only exceptions were Caleb and Joshua (Deuteronomy 1:29-32), who believed God would help Israel to take the Promised Land. Belief spurs on courage rather than cowardice; it incites faith rather than fear. Can you think of an opportunity you missed because of your fear? Fear has a way of keeping us from moving forward. And, just as there are consequences and missed opportunities when we fear, there are blessings when we don't fear. Caleb and Joshua had no fear and were the only two of the Israelites from Egypt who experienced the blessings of the Promised Land.

Blessings When We Don't Fear

What blessings might we experience when we don't give in to fear? Well, remember my fear of flying? After one of my books was published, my publisher wanted to send me on a two-week media tour that involved *a lot* of flying! Rather than refuse to fly, I decided to trust the Lord with whom I live and move and exist (Acts 17:28). During the trip, the Lord gave me many opportunities to minister to others, not only on television, but at the airport as I waited for my flights, and on the planes, too. My greatest joy was to share Christ with complete strangers. You never know how God might use your words (and His Word!) in another person's life (Isaiah 55:11). After the tour, I received e-mails from all over the United States, and one from India. Several people inquired further about how to have faith in Christ.

All this happened after I was willing to overcome my fear. The Lord really does put us back on the horse when we fall off. He does this by helping us confront our fears. For me, it was getting back on a plane. For Sheila, it was a tremendous fear of being alone at night. When she found out that her husband was going to be gone for several days, she panicked. She had never been alone. Someone had always been with her. So she called me and asked if I could spend a couple nights with her while her husband was gone.

Curious, I asked, "Why are you afraid of being home alone?"

"I fear having a diabetic attack, and what if no one is here to help me?" she replied.

I then asked, "Do you have diabetic attacks often?"

Sheila, who was 40, explained that she hadn't had an attack since she was a child. Wanting to help her, but not able to leave my young children, I invited Sheila to stay with me. But because I lived several hours away from her, Sheila turned down my offer. She was hesitant to drive alone.

Because Sheila couldn't find anyone to stay with her, we resolved that she would call me, regardless of the time, if she needed me, if she started feeling ill, if she had any fear. I then gave her the following verse to meditate upon:

> *Truly, the Lord's strength supplies all our needs according to His riches in glory and grace in Christ Jesus.*

> You will not be afraid of the terror by night, or of the arrow that flies by day; of the pestilence that stalks in darkness, or of the destruction that lays waste at noon....no evil will befall you, nor will any plague come near your tent (Psalm 91:5-6,10).

After those two nights passed, I got a call from Sheila, who said, "Donna, the last two nights have been the best I've ever had of learning to trust Jesus, and His Word." Sheila went on to explain how great she felt to be confronted with her fears, and with the help of Jesus, to face them head-on, and deal with them. She ended by saying, "I feel like a new woman!"

It's been said that fear can transform evil into good and danger into safety. And, as happened to Sheila, our deepest fear can be turned into our highest joy (Psalm 112:4). Truly, the Lord's strength supplies all our needs according to His riches in glory and grace in Christ Jesus.

The Promise of Strength

In 1932, John and Betty Stam, who were American missionaries in China, were kidnapped from their home. As they were dragged along a street, a postal worker saw them and frantically asked John, "Where are they taking you? Where are you going?"

John replied, "We do not know where they are going, but we are going to heaven."

No one could say such words without the Lord's strength upon him. God's strength can transform a discouraged person into a courageous one. The word courage comes from the Old French *corage*, based on the Latin root *cor*, which means "heart." It takes much heart to have the ability to move forward in the face of fear. To press on in the face of pain or grief. To act upon our beliefs despite the disapproval of others. All the godly people of the past—from the Old Testament to the New, from the bygone saints to the modern-day saints such as the Stams—have needed such strength to stay focused on God rather than on their fear. We too are to embrace this same strength (and tell others about it, too!— Isaiah 35:2).

So what is this divine strength? It is *courage that enables action*. Fear paralyzes us, whereas courage propels us to move forward in action. Such courage allows us to do *all* things (Philippians 4:13). We can step out in faith because we know God is with us (Isaiah 41:10). We can know God won't allow evil to touch us (Palm 91:10; 2 Thessalonians 3:3). Do you have the courage to trust God in all circumstances, even when circumstances don't look good? Do you have courage even when it seems as if God's protection is far from you?

The Promise of Protection

One morning, after walking Brian out to the car, giving him a kiss, and waving good-bye as he ventured off to work, I stood there and prayed for his safety:

> Dear Lord, You promise that You will give Your angels charge concerning Brian, and guard him *in all* his ways (Psalm 91:11). Please keep him away from all careless truck drivers, drunk drivers, drivers on drugs, drivers who aren't paying attention on the road, and reckless teenage drivers. Because of all the harm that could be brought to him this day, please have Your strong and competent angels surround the entire car. Thank You for Your promise of protection.

I have prayed this way, daily, for *years*, as Brian left for work, and for his drive back home. Well, one morning after I prayed I went back into the house, crashed on the couch, and reflected over my praying. I pondered out loud,

> Lord, do You really hear me? I'm sure You do; it's just that I pray each day over Brian, and I sometimes wonder if You would protect him regardless of my praying or not praying.

Not more than 15 minutes later, I got a phone call from my friend Traci. She said, "Donna, you aren't going to believe this. I was driving west and saw Brian approaching at a distance, driving east. A car behind me passed me up and *stayed* on Brian's side of the road and didn't return into its lane. I honestly couldn't see how Brian could possibly avoid being hit head-on by that car. Miraculously, he avoided being hit! It was obviously the Lord's protection."

About an hour later, when Brian arrived at work, he gave me a call. "Donna, you're not going to believe what happened to me." He then told me exactly what Traci had told me, and added, "I do not know how in this world I could have avoided being hit. I tried moving the car a bit, trying to avoid the guy, but honestly, I thought my life was over."

Brian then made a comment I've never forgotten: "Donna, it's because of your prayers that I'm alive this very moment."

What confirmation from the Lord! He *does* hear my prayers for protection, not only for Brian but also for so many others, including my nephew, Jonathan, whom I constantly prayed for while he served as a Marine in Iraq. He had some very close calls, including a failed terrorist roadside bomb blast on a road near the Syrian border. He received a Purple Heart medal after being injured in that blast. Had the blast detonated as planned, Jonathan and everyone with him would have been killed. But, God had His way.

I've come to discover that the evil one doesn't want us to fully accept God's protection for us or lean heavily upon that protection. How do I know this? Let's look at the Bible's account about Satan's temptation of Jesus in the wilderness. The devil said to Jesus, "It is written: He will command His angels concerning You to guard You...on their hands they will bear You up, so that you will not strike Your foot against a stone" (Luke 4:10; quoting from Psalm 91:11-12).

Do you notice what the devil intentionally left out when he quoted from Psalm 91? Let's take a closer look at what Scripture says: "For He will give His angels charge concerning you, *to guard you in all your ways.*" The devil doesn't want us to realize that our dear Lord will guard us in *all* our ways—not just in some ways, not just when He feels like it, but *always,* in every step we take. Satan would prefer we think of our safety as just a coincidence rather than the power of God at work. Our enemy keeps us down when he can successfully take our focus off such a tremendous promise as God's protection. We need to remember that the Lord will never act below Himself or be forgetful of His Word, on which we base our hope. When we trust what He says, such as "I will protect you," we can be free of worry.

God's Strength and Protection in the Midst of Problems

"But what about those times when Christians *do* get hurt?" you ask. "Does that mean God failed to keep His promise?"

It's true that sometimes it may *appear* as if God didn't keep His promise...but that's probably because we don't know the full story. For example, consider a friend of ours, who is also named Brian. He had a diabetic attack while driving and ended up in a terrible accident that nearly took his life. His nose, femur, pelvis, and back were broken. His bladder burst, and his face was damaged to the point of needing plastic surgery. He also had at least three blood transfusions. Pictures in the newspaper showed Brian to be a bloody mess when rescue workers got him out of his car. On the surface, it can appear as if God did not protect Brian *in all his ways.* Sure, we can say that God protected Brian from death, but why not from all harm? God could have done that. What most people don't know is what has been happening behind the scenes. With permission from Brian and his wife, Laurie, I'll share their story with you.

On the morning of the accident, Laurie was feeling a bit discouraged. She had gone outside to pray. In tears, she asked the Lord to help her to grow in her spiritual life, to help her just *surrender everything.* After her time of praying and expressing her desire for spiritual growth no matter what it took, she sensed an overwhelming peace. That peace would be the catalyst for strengthening Laurie for what was to come in just a few short hours.

What Laurie didn't know at the time she prayed was that her husband, Brian, was also praying. He, too, wanted to grow spiritually. "I was especially asking the Lord to help me to trust Him more," he said.

Through the accident, Laurie and Brian got their prayers answered. Not only is Laurie now able to surrender everything to the Lord, but Brian is able to fully trust God in all things. Countless times since the accident, the Lord has shown Brian that He will provide for Brian's needs—such as the money and food He provided during the time of Brian's recovery, when he was unable to work. Brian saw the Lord provide another car for him, for their only car had been demolished (two churches pitched in and bought the car). On and on the Lord's tender mercies were poured out upon Brian. The Lord also called Brian's attention to two life-changing facts. First, the importance of checking regularly his blood sugar levels. Although Brian felt just fine when he got into his car that morning, he had not been consistent in checking his blood sugar. Brian said, "I came to realize that what I do doesn't just affect me, it affects my family. Every decision I make, even to check or not check my blood sugar, affects them. My kids could have been without a father."

The second fact the Lord showed Brian was that he is dearly treasured by others. "After the accident, I came to see that my life did matter; that it did have an effect on other people's lives, in one way or another."

Through this accident, Brian and Laurie saw that "God causes all things to work together for good to those who love God, to those who are called according to His purpose" (Romans 8:28). Those long and hard months of recovery were not easy for Laurie and Brian, but because they had the peace of God, they could say, "The LORD is for me; I will not fear" (Psalm 118:6).

Like Brian and Laurie, we too can have peace when we *stay away from fear*. It's a peace that gives us tranquility of spirit, even during the greatest of trials. Consider how unheard of this divine peace is in the nonbelieving world. People cannot willingly submit to what they do not understand. They cannot imagine giving up pleasure, gain, health, and riches in exchange for pain, loss, disease, or car accidents.

We all need to live with the realization that we may have times of intense suffering come upon us. When that happens, will we still be able to say, "God is good"? If we face a painful loss, can we still say, "Blessed be His name"? This was the peace Brian and Laurie had as they abided in the perfect will of God. They knew God would bless and not curse. They understood that He rules from above as they "live and move and exist" in Him (Acts 17:28). They know that He truly protects.

Now, there are some very sincere Christians who believe that absolutely *no harm* should ever come to a believer. They believe that because "God is for us" (Romans 8:31), then life should be a bed of roses. Perhaps a man named Al Braca would disagree.

When the United States was attacked on 9/11, we heard stories about Christians dying alongside non-Christians. One pastor couldn't accept that God would allow these Christians to die. He preached, for example, that the only reason Christians died at the World Trade Center was because God had told them to leave their offices and go outside, but they didn't. Because they refused to listen to God, according to the pastor, they suffered the consequences.

I have to disagree—especially in light of the fact there were Christians who *intentionally* stayed behind so that they could share Christ with those who were stuck under debris and couldn't get out. I immediately think of Al Braca, who, knowing the danger he was in, called his wife on his cell phone and told her he was going to stay in the World Trade Center to share the gospel with 50 of his co-workers who were trapped. People like Al were not disobeying God; they were trusting His command, "Do not fear!" (Lamentations 3:57). Because of Al's lack of fear about what might happen to himself, he most assuredly was able to bring some people into the kingdom: "Greater love has no one than this, that one lay down his life for his friends" (John 15:13).

John 15:13 shows us that our spiritual fruitfulness has nothing to do with how many years we have here on earth. Rather, it's based on love, selflessness, and all that the Lord makes beautiful in us. This should mean much more to us than a long life, or a life without trouble.

Years ago when at a women's conference, I listened to a then-70-year-old Elisabeth Elliot say, "I am ready to see my Lord." Why could she say this? Because there comes a time when the bright hope of heaven means so much more than anything here on earth—especially when you feel that you've accomplished all that the Lord has called you to do.

So yes, difficulties will come to us...especially because we are the enemy of the devil. Who can tell what losses and disappointments await us? Who can count on continued health or prosperity? Who can tell what the next turn in the road bears for us? Who can be assured against calamity or sudden death? No one other than God can answer those questions.

The Lord never promised us that He'll keep us from suffering, or that we'll have a trouble-free life. Rather, He promised to provide His grace to us in the midst of suffering: "I will *strengthen* you, surely I will *help* you, surely I will *uphold you* with my righteous right hand" (Isaiah 41:10).

Safe in His Hand

The Bridegroom *will not* lose what He values most—you, His bride. Refusing to lose you, He died for you. And, just as He promised to be with Abraham (Genesis 21:22), Jacob (Genesis 28:15), Joseph (Genesis 39:2), and Samuel (1 Samuel 3:19), so He promises to always be with you—to go behind you, as well as before you (Psalm 139:5), and to protect you in all your ways (Psalm 91:11; 121:8).

And so it is, that in the hours of darkness and disappointment, when fear is tempted to surface, you can put yourself in the palm of our Beloved's hand. There, you are safe and secure. No one can ever take you out of His grip (John 10:28-29). Because He's always with you, though devastation may one day come, you will face it with Him at your side, and it will not destroy you:

> Do not be afraid of sudden fear. When you pass through the waters, I will be with you; and through the rivers, they will not overflow you. When you walk through the fire, you will not be scorched, nor will the flame burn you. You will fear disaster no more. For I am the Lord your God...your Savior.... You are precious in My sight...you are honored and I love you.... Do not fear, for I am with you (based on Proverbs 3:25; Isaiah 42:2-5; Zephaniah 3:15).

What comforting words from the One who obviously loves and cares so much for you! He doesn't want you, or me, to live in fear, in distress, or in anguish...and that's why He repeatedly tells us to not be afraid, but to trust in Him.

Our Lord not only protects you and makes you His own, but also gives you His splendor: "...on account of your beauty, for it was perfect because of My splendor which I bestowed on you" (Ezekiel 16:14). This divine splendor, which beautifies you, shows no fear, but rather, takes comfort in our Bridegroom's vows of "I will."

I will never desert you,
nor will I forsake you;
I will deliver you.
I will set you securely on high.

You will call Me, and *I will* answer you.
I will help you in trouble;
I will rescue and honor you.
With a long life *I will* satisfy you.
I will go before you and make the rough places smooth,
I will set you in safety for which you long,
I will abundantly bless you.
Therefore, do not fear, for I am with you;
do not be dismayed, for I am your God.
I will strengthen you and help you;
I will uphold you with my righteous right hand.[4]

Our Passion in Action

1. What are some ways fear can keep us from being spiritually passionate?

2. Fear got the best of Ahaz (Isaiah 7:2). What did the Lord tell Ahaz through Isaiah (Isaiah 7:4)? Rather than take heed to God's word, what did Ahaz do instead (2 Kings 16:1-4; 16:7-8)? What were the consequences of Ahaz's fear (see 2 Kings 16:6; 16:6,8-9; 2 Chronicles 28:5-6,19)? What consequences could come to your life if you don't give up your fear(s)?

3. What one thing *must* we fear (Psalm 147:11)? How does that fear differ from the fears we should banish from our lives? What do we gain when we fear the Lord (Psalm 111:10)? What does this extra benefit provide (see Psalm 54:6; Proverbs 8:12-13; 14:27; 16:6; Ecclesiastes 5:1)? What other benefits do we have in fearing the Lord (Psalm 112:1,6-8)? Will such fear ever stop (see Revelation 19:5)? It's been said that when we fear God, we fear nothing else. Why is this statement true?

4. People react differently to bad news. Let's consider three examples: Daniel, Job, and Jesus. When Daniel found out about the document prompted by his enemies, what was his reaction (see the meaning of this document in Daniel 6:12, and his reaction to the document in Daniel 6:10)? What bad news did Job receive (Job 1:12-19)? What was his reaction (Job 1:20-22)? What was Jesus' reaction to the bad news of Lazarus' death (John 11:35)?

5. When God's messengers were sent to deliver news, what were always their first words (Matthew 1:20; Luke 1:11-13,30; Acts 27:23-24)? When bad news comes, how should we react (Psalm 112:7)?

6. When the Assyrian army threatened to conquer Hezekiah's kingdom, Hezekiah chose to fear the Lord instead of the Assyrian army. What blessing did Hezekiah receive as a result (see 2 Kings 18:5-7)? What blessings could come to your life as you turn your fear or discouragement over to Jesus? This week, start praying for God to help you resolve your fear.

7. When we eliminate fear, what do we become (Psalm 27:3)? What are we able to endure (Psalm 27:3; 46:2)? Who can harm us (Psalm 118:6; Hebrews 13:6)?

8. Can God ever be absent from your life (see Deuteronomy 31:6; Joshua 1:5; Hebrews 13:5)? How does knowing this help you in your current circumstances?

3

The Promise of Provision for Your Every Need

"If you ask anything in My name, I will do it."
—JOHN 14:14

Over 21 years ago, when living the "single life," my roommate Kathy was going through some struggles. She really needed encouragement. As I prayed for her, the Lord put it on my heart to take her out to dinner as a way of cheering her up. At the time, I was what you would call a poor starving student and lived on a very tight budget. But despite my budget, I wanted to obey what I believed was the Lord's prompting.

Pulling up to the restaurant with Kathy, I silently prayed, *Lord, You know my financial situation. I'm trusting You with this.*

Kathy and I went in and sat in a cushioned booth. Getting comfortable, we eventually ordered our dinner. While waiting for the meal, we talked about some of the trials Kathy was experiencing. All of a sudden, Kathy gasped. Staring right at me, she exclaimed, "Donna, don't move!"

Freezing up, I asked, "Why shouldn't I move?"

Laughing hard, she replied, "Because right on the back of your seat is a huge cockroach!"

Instantly, my reflexes kicked in. I screamed and jumped out of the booth. This, of course, caught the attention of everyone in the restaurant. The waitress came and asked what the problem was. I then pointed it out to her.

The waitress took a cloth napkin and with it, snatched our unwelcome visitor.

I then sat back down, and Kathy and I resumed our conversation. A few minutes later the waitress came by and said, "The manager would like to offer you sodas on the house."

We both looked at each other, and then at the waitress. We cheerfully said, "Thanks!"

Later, the waitress came back and said, "The manager would like to offer you dessert, on the house."

Again, we told her, "Thanks!"

A few minutes later she came again and said, "The manager would like for you to have your entire meal on the house."

We were thrilled, and once again thanked the waitress, and told her to thank the manager.

I learned a few lessons that evening. One, the Lord had provided more than just food for Kathy and me. He had given me an opportunity to trust Him more—in this case, for His provision. I also learned God can use even the yuckiest of things, the most troubling of things, to bring about His provision. He does indeed promise us that He *will* provide— He just doesn't tell us *how* He will provide. I would never have imagined that the Great Provider (*Jehovah-Jireh*, as stated in the Bible, which means "the Lord provides") would take Kathy and me out to dinner, and pay for it with a cockroach!

Corrie ten Boom, while in a Nazi concentration camp, couldn't have imagined that God would provide lice as a way to keep German officers out of the barrack she shared with other prisoners. The lice were what enabled Corrie and her sister, Betsy, to have Bible studies for the other women and lead some of them to Christ.

And remember when Elijah was without food? He never would have guessed that the Lord would use ravens—those large black birds—to deliver him bread and meat morning and night (1 Kings 17:6).

Then there was the blind man in John chapter 8, who was healed by Jesus. The Lord provided sight for him with the use of dirt and saliva (verse 6).

Cockroaches, lice, ravens, dirt, and saliva. Yes! Like providing a flower among weeds or a stream in a desert, our God does provide, in creative ways, and sometimes in painful ways. And it's this thought, that pain could be part of God's provision, that many of us don't want to accept. Actually, such a concept as pain being "loving" is a great hindrance for many of us when it comes to thinking about the Great Provider. But really, pain is a beneficial provision because it can result in spiritual growth.

The Painful but Loving Ways of God

Allowing Hardship for Our Good

On Christmas evening in 1983, I was driving to Brian's sister's house (Barbara Anne) to meet with family. During the drive, I had a wonderful time of prayer. Just a few blocks from the house, I made a sincere plea to the Lord, "Please, do *whatever* You need to do in my life to keep my eyes on You." Literally moments later, a drunk driver came speeding right at me, hitting the door right next to me. A stranger rushed to the scene and yelled out, "Can I call anyone for you?" I was able to hand him a piece of paper, which I had earlier placed on the passenger seat, with Barbara Anne's phone number on it.

Within minutes, Brian and paramedics were at the scene. Someone told Brian, "With an accident of this magnitude, she'll probably be paralyzed." After the paramedics expended quite a bit of effort to get me out of the car, I was able to stand up and stumble around on my own. Amazed, the paramedics still thought I needed care and wanted to take me to the hospital. I insisted I would be fine, and assured them that Brian could take me. In the emergency room, physicians checked me over and removed glass from my head and ears. I was told that I had a concussion and would have to stay at home, bedridden—which I did for close to two weeks.

Now a nonbeliever might say, "That's what you get for making such a prayer request!" But those of us who have been with Jesus for a while know that He doesn't answer our prayers with vengeance. He always has our best in mind. In this case, I don't blame God for causing the accident, but I understand He allowed it, and indeed, it was for my good. During that time in bed, the Lord gave me plenty of time to reflect. I spent *lots* of time in His Word, and through the Word, He showed me areas in which I needed to grow in my life. While I didn't like the pain or enjoy having a mangled car, I can say wholeheartedly that the accident was definitely a catalyst that helped to get my eyes evermore on Jesus. Hymn writer John Newton put it this way:

> I asked the Lord that I might grow,
> In faith and love, and every grace,
> Might more of His salvation know,
> And seek more earnestly His face.
>
> I hoped that in some favored hour,
> At once He'd answer my request.
> And by His love's constraining power,
> Subdue my sins and give me rest.
>
> Instead of this, He made me feel,
> The hidden evils of my heart.
> And let the angry powers of hell,
> Assault my soul in every part.

Yes, more with His own hand He seemed,
Intent to aggravate my woe.
Crossed all the fair designs I schemed,
Blasted my gourds, and laid me low.

"Lord, why is this?" I trembling cried,
"Will You pursue Your worm to death?"
"This is the way," the Lord replied,
"I answer prayer for grace and strength."

"These inward trials I employ,
From self, and pride, to set you free;
And break your schemes of earthly joy,
That you may find your all in Me."[1]

That statement "That you may find your all in Me" is beautiful, isn't it? And as women growing in spiritual passion, we long for that. But, can't we find our all in Him without the suffering? Certainly, we would prefer to go through life untouched by sorrows. But, that's not reality. We know from Scripture that life does have its joys, but it also has its griefs. There's the story of Ruth and Naomi, in which Naomi lost her husband and two sons (Ruth 1:2-5). There's the apostle Paul praying three times for the "thorn" in his flesh to be healed—and it never was.

And, as we travel through the Psalms, we see time and again that the psalmists experienced loneliness and rejection.

> *Beneath all our trials, sorrows, and struggles, our Beloved is at work to help us grow in greater spiritual passion.*

Time will only tell when sorrow will write its experiences on our brow. I already get teary-eyed at the thought of my children leaving home and going off to college. And just the other day Brian and I were talking about how difficult it's going to be when the first one of us is taken to our *real* home. For myself, I can only imagine how hard it's going to be, being left in a home without familiar faces that once filled all the rooms with joy.

Yes, life will present us with very lonely and empty times. But beneath all our trials, sorrows, and struggles, our Beloved is at work to help us grow in greater spiritual passion. He will do whatever it takes to get us there. And here's our comfort. *Jesus will never permit an evil to befall you or me* unless it's to prevent a greater evil.

Allowing Evil to Prevent a Greater Evil

Look at the evil that came upon Joseph. His brothers, who were jealous of him, ruthlessly threw him into an empty well, and then sold him into slavery (Genesis 37:1-36). While the brothers' actions were evil, God worked through that circumstance—and others—to eventually put Joseph in one of the highest positions of authority in Egypt. Years later, when Joseph came face-to-face with his brothers again, he said to them,

> Do not be angry with yourselves, because you sold me here, *for God sent me here before you to preserve life.* ...God sent me before you to preserve for you a remnant in the earth, and to keep you alive by a great deliverance. Now, therefore, it was not you who sent me here, but God; and He has made me a father to Pharaoh and lord of all his household and ruler over all the land of Egypt (Genesis 45:5,7-8).

Joseph exalted in the good that occurred. Certainly others, including his brothers, had done evil against him, and however wrong that was, had it not occurred, there would have been a greater evil of lives lost. It was because of Joseph's position in Egypt that the Jewish people were able to move to Egypt, where they could get food. Otherwise, they all would have died in the famine in their homeland.

When Corrie ten Boom was placed in a concentration camp, that was indeed an evil. But, God allowed that evil to occur in Corrie's life to prevent others from experiencing the greater evil of hell, which was made possible when Corrie and her sister led others to Christ. Can you think of an evil that was done against you in the past, but greater good came as a result of it?

Samuel, the Israeli judge, was so focused upon God's faithful provision for good that he prayed, "Do as You have spoken" (2 Samuel 7:25). Samuel trusted whichever way God answered his prayer. He knew that ultimately God would provide that which was good (2 Samuel 7:28). Romans 8:28 tells us, "God causes all things to work together for good to those who love God." Jesus is the Giver, and we are the receiver. We, the taker, cry out, "I need." He, the Supplier, answers, "I have." Jesus said, "Ask me anything...I will do it" (John 14:14). But, does Jesus really mean that we can ask Him for *anything*?

What If Jesus Provided Whatever We Asked of Him?

Remember the two sons of Zebedee, James and John? They asked Jesus, "Teacher, we want You to do for us whatever we ask of You" (Mark 10:35).

Jesus inquired, "What do you want Me to do for you?" (verse 36).

They replied, "Grant that we may sit, one on Your right and one on Your left, in Your glory" (verse 37).

Jesus must have been shocked at their bold request. He said to them, almost as a warning, "You do not know what you are asking" (verse 38). He continued, "Are you able to drink the cup that I drink, or to be baptized with the baptism with which I am baptized?"

If Jesus were to grant James' and John's request, they would have to drink a cup filled with suffering (Mark 14:36), and experience the baptism of death (Luke 12:50). Obviously, these men had no idea what they were asking for.

Consider Moses, who asked of the Lord: "So if You are going to deal thus with me, please kill me at once, if I have found favor in Your sight, and do not let me see my wretchedness" (Numbers 11:15). Moses didn't really know what he was asking. Rather than fulfill Moses' request, God brought relief to his burdened heart by giving him the assistance of 70 elders (Numbers 11:16-17).

Elijah prayed, "It is enough; now, O LORD, take my life, for I am not better than my fathers" (1 Kings 19:4). Elijah, too, didn't know what he was asking. Rather than answer this prayer, the Lord provided an angel to refresh Elijah (1 Kings 19:5-8).

Jonah prayed in a similar way as Moses and Elijah: "O LORD, please take my life from me, for death is better to me than life" (Jonah 4:3). Unlike Moses and Elijah, Jonah prayed with a rebellious heart. You see, God had told Jonah to reach out to the people of Nineveh with His truth. Jonah was quite angry about this. He didn't believe these godless people deserved such a chance at salvation. The Lord dealt with Jonah's anger by allowing a plant to swiftly grow and give Jonah shade from the hot sun, but then allowed a worm to quickly eat the plant away. This made Jonah even more upset. God then showed Jonah that he seemed to care more for a mere plant than for the lost people of Nineveh (see Jonah 4:1-11).

> God answers our prayers according to His infinite wisdom rather than our limited foresight.

Perhaps you know about Augustine's mother, Maria, who prayed for her son not to go to Rome. She feared he would get into trouble there. Fortunately, the Lord didn't answer Maria's prayer. It was in Rome that Augustine came to Christ and served Him from that day till his death.

We can be thankful that the Lord doesn't always answer our prayers according to our wishes. He answers them according to His infinite wisdom rather than our limited foresight. And, when He answers, He's interested in seeing our will align with His will. As 1 John 5:14 says, "If we ask anything according to *His will*, He hears us." It's not that God turns a deaf ear to some of our prayers. Rather, He always answers in a manner consistent with His will.

For example, if we ask Him to make us rich, and that's not in our best interest, then He *will not* make us rich. If we ask to marry a certain man, and God knows he wouldn't be best for us, then He *will not* provide that person. Of course, we can go against God's will, but then we will suffer the consequences of our disobedience. By contrast, if we ask for spiritual riches, God will indeed provide them, because such a request aligns beautifully with His will that we

> be filled with the knowledge of His will in all spiritual wisdom and understanding, so that you may walk in a manner worthy of the Lord, to please Him in all respects, bearing fruit in every good work and increasing in the knowledge of God; strengthened with all power, according to His glorious might, for the attaining of all steadfastness and patience; joyously giving thanks to the Father, who has qualified us to share in the inheritance of the saints in Light (Colossians 1:9-12).

When we are in prayer, and in the Word, we will be filled with the knowledge of God's will. The Holy Spirit also shows us God's will, through the prompting of our heart and leading us in the way we should go. We must be loyal to His inward leading. And sometimes instead of leading us, He will stop us, making it apparent what He doesn't want us to do.

Both Brian and I have experienced many shut doors. Both he and I, when single, and then during the early years of our marriage, had vigorously pursued the mission field, believing that's what the Lord wanted of us. Yet despite being accepted for ministry in Holland, some events and circumstances clearly closed the door for us. Not giving up, we began to pursue ministry in Albania. This time the door was not only shut, but it was locked and the key thrown away. I prayed, "Lord, at a time when so many people are refusing to go to the mission field, why would You close the door on people who are so willing to go?" To this day I don't fully understand God's answer. But it's not for me to question Him. Rather, I need to trust He knows what He is doing.

The Lord may not only shut the door on major decisions in your life, He can also shut the door on more minor decisions in order to protect us. Before we had Michelle and Johnathan, I worked outside the home. One evening, on my way home from work, I planned to go grocery shopping. Just before getting off the freeway exit, I received the strongest prompting from the Lord *not* to go to the store. I remember praying aloud, "But Lord, I've got to go home and cook dinner, and my cupboards are bare." Again, I was prompted *not* to go to the store. So I didn't.

A little over an hour later, Brian came home. I apologized to him for not having any food in the house and explained to him why I hadn't gone to the store. Brian's face turned pale, and he sat on the couch, and for a moment was completely silent. Feeling badly, I said, "I guess you're pretty hungry, huh?"

Brian looked at me and said, "I take it you didn't hear."

Puzzled, I asked, "Hear what?"

"About an hour ago, three gunmen went into and terrorized that very store. They demanded that everyone stop their shopping and get facedown on the floor. One of the thugs put a gun to the skull of a cashier while he demanded the money. When the gunman got what they wanted, they fled. Thankfully, no one was killed."

The Lord did indeed "shut the door" for me to go shopping, and I am so thankful He had. He knows not only the present, but also the future. He, and only He, knows what's truly best. That's why we can rest in His will. If He answers "No," we can be just as content as if He answered "Yes." And even if the Lord hadn't warned me, and I had gone into the grocery store, then He would have had a purpose for me being there as well.

This is true even when horrible things *do* happen, even though we don't understand why. For example, over 20 years ago, Brian's friend Tim was working in a grocery store when a robbery took place. As Tim rushed to help a cashier who was being harassed by a gunman, he was shot and killed. Tim was a very strong Christian who had lived a godly life worth admiring and following. The gunman was caught and put in prison. Tim's father then visited the prison and shared Christ with the very man who killed his son. While an evil deed had been done, a greater evil could be avoided by others if they became Christians. At Tim's funeral, the gospel was again presented. So, even in death—*our death*—God's good will and purposes will be fulfilled, for the greater good of God's glory.

And so it is that if we pray according to God's will, He will hear us. "And if we know that He hears us in whatever we ask, we know that we have the requests which we have asked from Him" (1 John 5:15). Such a promise as this certainly helps us rest in God's will.

Resting in God's Will

I like to think about heaven a lot and about what our brothers and sisters in Christ who have gone before us are doing up there this very moment. And as I imagine their glorious life in the kingdom, I have no difficulty imagining them living in the will of God. They would do *anything* for Jesus. They know His will is good. No matter what God asks, they wouldn't question Him because they rest in His will and good pleasure. As a result, can you imagine the spiritual passion that fills up heaven? As much as is possible, being in this sinful world, we too can have such heavenly passion. It occurs when we, like the saints in heaven, have completely forgotten about our own lives because the will of God is our complete focus. We don't think of danger, scorn, or opposition because we desire to glory in God's will.

Consider Martin Luther, the former Catholic priest who helped start the Reformation. During his journey to Worms, Germany, to face the religious powers that be, friends stopped him on the dusty roads, begging him not to go. Luther refused to be swayed. Closer to Worms, Luther's friend Spalatin begged him to not go into Worms, warning him in the harshest terms that his life was in danger. Luther answered that he would go to Worms even "if there were as many devils as there are tiles on the roofs."[2]

Only God could have provided such determination in Luther. And so too did He provide the same determination in Paul, who said, "I am ready not only to be bound, but even to die at Jerusalem for the name of the Lord Jesus" (Acts 21:13).

When we pray for and seek the Lord's will in our lives, He will provide for us the determination to fulfill His will. In our mind, this determination silences all objections to what we are doing; it even suppresses our own thoughts as we focus upon thoughts of God alone. Let me illustrate what I mean.

God Provides the Determination

Years before I married or even dated Brian (although we were friends), I was engaged to a seminary student whom I'll call Eric. The night we were to go out to a nice dinner and to buy engagement/wedding rings, the Lord got my attention. I almost felt as if the gates of heaven had opened wide and someone shouted, "Don't do it!" I was quite startled by this, but the Spirit of God just kept pounding this message over and over upon my heart: "Don't do it!"

In prayer, I said, "Lord, I have no reason not to marry Eric. He's a godly man; he loves You tremendously. Why would You not want me to marry him?"

It didn't seem the Lord was giving me any clear answers. That didn't matter. All I knew for certain was that I had to pay attention to the all-knowing Spirit—otherwise, I would be in disobedience. I asked the Lord for confirmation of what I was doing. I asked Him to help this man be calm and understanding as I expressed my concern. I also asked for the determination, a firmness of purpose, to do as I believed He was asking me to do. With conviction that the Lord was moving mightily, I got out of my dressy clothes and into my casuals.

When Eric came over to the house, he was dressed in a suit, and handed me a bouquet of flowers. He then asked, "Why are you still in your jeans?"

I asked Eric to sit on the couch, and I told him what had just happened. Although he did ask quite a few questions (understandably), he did accept my words very calmly and with much understanding. That was my confirmation from the Lord that I was indeed going in the direction He wanted me to go in.

Abiding in God's will isn't easy. Believe me, as I peeked out the window and watched Eric walk away, I was tempted to call him back. But, I had to be resolute. That's what living out God's will requires: being firm in conviction that we obey God, regardless of our feelings. Now, abiding in God's will doesn't take away the pain; the breakup tore my heart apart, and the loss was real because our two-year relationship had been real. *What will life be without Eric?* I asked myself. I didn't know what the future held, but I knew that if the Lord had prompted me to break up, He would guide my next steps—whatever they might be.

In the days afterward, word of the breakup got around fast. Friends came over to my apartment or called me on the phone. They all asked the same question—though they seemed to already know the answer: "Are you crazy?" I knew my friends were only trying to help. One friend said, "Donna, you've always wanted to be a pastor's wife, and here's your great chance. You're throwing it away!"

Another friend said, "Eric is one of the most handsome guys I've ever seen. Why give up that hunk?"

Still another said, "Donna, you're no spring chicken. This is probably your last chance at getting married."

I received many other comments. And, while it's good to receive advice, we must make sure that it aligns with the Word of God. My friends couldn't show me that I was out of God's will in breaking up with Eric. Thankfully, as the days went on, the Lord clearly showed me I was indeed in His will with the breakup—and that it was for the best for the both of us.

In due time, the Lord will reveal to each and every one of us why He does what He does. The snow won't hide the flowers forever—eventually you will see the flowers. And what flowers did I see? I saw an entire bouquet of daisies—and one single rose. That rose has to do with a man named Brian Morley. During the two years I was dating Eric, I had *no idea whatsoever* that Brian was praying one simple prayer in regard to me: "Lord, if it's not your will for Donna to one day marry Eric, can I get a chance at dating her?"

Brian thought his prayer wouldn't be answered when, just a week before the breakup, Eric had told Brian we were engaged. God certainly works in mysterious ways, doesn't He?

Thy Will Be Done

When our motto and heart's desire is "Your will be done, on earth as it is in heaven" (Matthew 6:10), Jesus will be standing right alongside us, providing for us the determination to face and endure all opposition, temptation, and even the weakness of our own heart.

When our motto and our heart's desire is "Thy will be done," it is so much easier to rest in the good pleasure of God's will—to see His goodness, and gratefully adore Him because of it.

When our motto and our heart's desire is "Thy will be done," we become perfectly content with what God wills for us. We can't help but give Him all our devotion and energy. This includes having a heavenly mind-set that makes us want to *do anything* for Jesus. *What spiritual passion!* Such passion believes in the promises of our Lord's provision.

Accepting Whatever Happens to Us

According to Steven Pybrum, author of *Money and Marriage*, one of the main reasons people divorce is because of money issues. This isn't just a problem with non-Christians, but with Christians as well. One Christian woman told me her reason for divorcing her husband was that "he's never been a good provider."

When I pointed out to her that she had a roof over her head and food in her refrigerator, she replied, "That's not enough. I want more, and I didn't sign up for the life my husband has given me and the kids."

Sadly, this woman was no more concerned about her earthly marriage than she was concerned about her marriage bond to Jesus. Along with her earthly husband, it was as if she had lost all respect for her heavenly husband, Jesus. She no longer trusted Him or had confidence in His provision for her. And, like her earthly marriage, her heavenly marriage had become bitter and distant. She couldn't love and revere Jesus, so she couldn't accept the life He was offering her. As a result, I saw in that woman "the strength of sin" breaking up both her earthly relationship with her husband and her heavenly marriage with Jesus.

Those of us who take our marriage bond with Jesus seriously know all that He has done for us (2 Corinthians 8:9). His love for us is greater than the love of a friend, a brother, or a father. He has shown us the love of a husband who offers complete provision. For our husband, Jesus, if He be worthy of the name, will share His lot with His wife. And, if we, His bride, are worthy of His name, we will accept *whatever* that lot is. If Jesus must suffer hardship, we should expect Him to share that with us. If He must live poorly here on earth, we should expect that, too.

We know Jesus loves us. We are content with not only His provision, but with the way He provides, however difficult that may be. We can be assured that "He who promised is faithful" (Hebrews 10:23). We will never lack anything, and all our needs will be met "according to His riches in glory in Christ Jesus" (Philippians 4:19). What incredible love Jesus has, to not only supply us all that we need, but to sacrifice everything, including His life, that we may be rich! "He was rich, yet for your sake He became poor, so that you through *His poverty* might become rich" (2 Corinthians 8:9).

Be encouraged. Because you are the bride of Christ, *He will surely take care of you!*

Our Passion in Action

1. What does the Bible say about prayer? (see Mark 11:24). How should we pray (see Matthew 6:10; Mark14:36)?

2. Have you ever received an answer to prayer that was completely unexpected...an answer similar to a cockroach, lice, or mud? Have you had an answer to prayer that was emotionally or physically painful for you? Have you ever lifted up a request that you are now glad God didn't answer?

3. In what ways has God helped you spiritually as He answers your prayers?

4. Read 1 Thessalonians 5:18. What is God's will for us—especially when we struggle with His provision or lack thereof?

5. What are four reasons we are to give thanks (see Luke 17:11-19; John 11:41-42; Colossians 3:15-17; 1 Thessalonians 5:11-13)? How might we show an attitude of gratitude for God's provision in our lives? How might we use our thankful spirit to strengthen another believer? How might our witness of a thankful spirit help an unbeliever?

4

The Promise of an Everlasting Love

"I have loved you with an everlasting love."
—JEREMIAH 31:3

One beautiful November day, Brian and I were driving toward Malibu Beach. On the windy road to the ocean, I silently looked out the window, observing the luscious green trees. In my mind, I was planning my breakup "speech." Brian and I had gotten back together nine months earlier (having dated off and on for several years prior). While we had always enjoyed a great friendship, it seemed that our dating was going to continue on *forever* while Brian continued his education (eventually completing three master's degrees and a doctorate!).

I really didn't know where this "bachelor till the rapture" stood anyway. He never told me that he loved me—that was reserved for whomever he would marry—*if* he was ever to marry. I had just been accepted as a missionary to be sent out by my church (which Brian didn't know yet), and I figured I needed to pursue the path the Lord seemed to have opened for me—to be a single missionary.

Once we got to the beautiful, endless shores of Malibu Beach, we went to an elegant restaurant and sat next to a huge window that gave us an awesome "outdoor" feeling. The waves were lapping near the window, and the sun was slowly setting, casting a colorful array of color across the sky.

After dinner, while there was still some daylight, we strolled out on the pier and made small talk. It was beginning to get a bit cold. Brian assisted me with putting on my sweater and said, "Isn't that sunset majestic?" Preoccupied more and more with my breakup speech, I simply replied, "Yes, majestic."

Brian then said, "Look at all those seagulls flocking together!"

I said, "Umm, yes, there's lots of birds."

As Brian was about to bring to my attention to yet another feature about the beautiful world around us, I interrupted, and with all the courage I could muster up, said, "Brian, I need to say something important."

Brian looked me in the eyes and said, "Let me say something first. Donna, I love you. I have for a long time."

Brian began to talk more and more about his love for me, and as he spoke with eloquence, I was getting quite confused. Thoughts were swirling in my mind, and it seemed as if Brian's words were echoing in the background. I then heard the words, "Will you marry me?"

Those words—"I love you...Will you marry me?"—came as a complete shock. I wasn't expecting this whatsoever! Rather than respond positively to such a wonderful turn of events, I felt a sudden urge to regurgitate my dinner. The only words I could manage to say, which surprised both of us, were "I think I'm going to throw up!"

Now it was Brian's turn to be shocked. For nearly three months, he had been dropping what he thought were clear hints of his interest in me—hints I *never* picked up. Brian thought, *How could Donna have such a reaction?*

Not wanting to put emotional pressure on me, Brian had decided beforehand to suggest I pray about his proposal for three days and then give him my answer—which I excitedly did on Thanksgiving Day.

Looking back on that beautiful day in Malibu, I wish I had responded differently. If I had just picked up on Brian's hints, I certainly would never have prepared a breakup speech. I would have anticipated a future of pursuing ministry as a couple. I also would have enjoyed what Brian tried to have—a romantic moment. But at least I can say I delighted in Brian's words of love. I admit that I was, and still am, in wonderment and astonishment that he would love me, of all people. After accepting his proposal, I looked forward to discovering his love for a lifetime.

As much as I am thankful for Brian's love, I am even more grateful for the love that Jesus has shown to me. How about you? Consider. You are an object of His lovingkindness. The word "lovingkindness," in the Old Testament, is the Hebrew word *hesed*,[1] and from what I could count, it's used 183 times.[2] The word literally speaks of zeal towards the one who is loved.[3] It also expresses a "belonging together,"[4] and it's a love "freely given."[5]

So imagine a man you've loved for years finally declaring his love for you with great zeal, telling you that you both belong together, and from that moment on, freely giving himself to you. I doubt you would feel like vomiting. You would be *ecstatic*. Well, this is what our God, our Bridegroom, is saying to you. His lovingkindness toward you is an intimate expression of His deep love for you. It means He's zealous for you; He believes you and He belong together; He is giving Himself freely to you. He is giving you His love—for eternity. It's impossible for His love to stop or to fade away. His love is here to stay.

His love is far richer than any human love. Who can fully comprehend "the breadth and length and height and depth" of Christ's love (Ephesians 3:18)? Who can truly "know the love of Christ which surpasses knowledge" (Ephesians 3:19)? The apostle Paul says those who have Christ dwelling in their hearts through faith (Ephesians 3:17) *can know and should know* Christ's love that we "may be filled up to all the fullness of God" (Ephesians 3:19). In other words, when we *really know*

God's eternal love for us, we will have an inner drive to passionately live out that love, to dwell in that love (1 John 4:16), and to be excited, like a bride is toward her groom—and this is a Groom who is "able to do far more abundantly beyond all that we can ask or think" (Ephesians 3:20).

While all this talk about God's love is wonderful, sadly but true, some women have a hard time fully accepting His love. They want His love, but…something or other gets in the way. For instance, some Christian women have a wrong view of God's love. Others, because of suffering, can't believe God loves them. Others, because of previous sin, believe God can't love them the same as He did before they sinned. Still others can't believe God loves them because no one ever has. But none of these hindrances should be allowed to block His love. Let's look more closely at each one and see how they can be overcome.

Wrong Views of God's Love

When I first came to Christ, I was thrilled about God's love for me. I wanted others to experience the same love, so I started sharing about it with a 20-year-old named Sherry. Sherry stopped me mid-sentence and said, in a condescending voice, "Yeah, I've heard about God's love all my life. I made a commitment to Christ as a child. But you know, I no longer believe He is a God of love."

I could hear a lot of hurt in Sherry's voice, so I asked, "What was it that took this glorious truth away from you?"

Sherry then told me her very sad story. Her father, a pastor of a church, had molested her and her sister for years. Sherry talked to her mother about it, but her mother refused to believe it. Her mother also said not to talk about it to anyone at the church.

Sherry told me she could remember many times being molested by her father during the week, and then hearing her father talk about God's love on Sunday morning.

In a dead tone, she said, "I see Christ's love as I see my father's love—empty."

There are many women who connect the treatment they received from their earthly father with the treatment they can expect from God. If their father was harsh, they view God as harsh. If their father was absent in their lives, then they view God as absent. If their father was a liar, so too is God. If only they could realize the truth of the Father's love! Jesus Himself confirms the Father's love: "The Father Himself loves you, because you have loved Me, and have believed that I came forth from the Father" (John 16:27).

Because God is love, and because He loves us intimately, He hates the horrible treatment we receive from others, especially when it comes from an earthly father. Such sin against us is especially a sin against God (Psalm 51:4).

If you struggle because of the lack of love you've received from your earthly father or others, I encourage you to begin discovering the truth of God's love. Start by looking at how different God's love is from an earthly father's love. He says, "My loving-kindness will not be removed from you" (Isaiah 54:10; see also Psalm 27:10), and His love is sacrificial—He was willing to send His only begotten Son to die for you (John 3:16). Even the best of earthly fathers cannot begin to compare to our heavenly Father!

While we may be bitter because of what an earthly father or any other person has done, we cannot hold on to that. In the same way God forgives us, we are called to forgive others: "Be kind to one another, tenderhearted, forgiving each other, just as God in Christ also has forgiven you" (Ephesians 4:32). As we learned in chapter 1, we're to forgive others. If we don't, we will live in bitterness—and bitterness and love cannot live side by side in the same heart. This kills the soul like nothing else! Let us, therefore, forgive and draw closer to Jesus: "Nearer, my God, to Thee, nearer to Thee! Even though it be a cross that raiseth me; still all my song shall be, nearer, my God, to thee, nearer, my God, to Thee, nearer to Thee."[6]

When Mourning Sets In

As of a few weeks ago at the time of this writing, 70-year-old Helen was diagnosed with breast cancer. Unfortunately the cancer has spread, and her prognosis doesn't look good. Prior to finding out about her cancer, Helen had prayed that God would keep her healthy so that she could care for Jim, her dying husband, who is quite bitter against God. Now Helen is being told that soon she won't have much strength left to care for Jim. Helen is fighting the urge to ask, "Why?" While she isn't outwardly questioning God's love (perhaps out of a sense of duty or fear), inwardly she's struggling to believe that He is good and has the good of His children in mind. Those who know Helen well say she says one thing outwardly, but feels something completely different inwardly. What a heavy burden she carries—all because she can't seem to understand God's goodness and love. My heart breaks for Helen and Jim...and for the many others who feel pressed down by the weight of disappointments, troubles, sorrows, and afflictions. They need our prayers and compassion.

Most people, as long as they are happy, will believe God loves them. But when problems set in, they no longer believe God's love even exists. However, theologian Charles Hodge remarked over a century ago that happiness is no proof of God's love.[7] Hodge also said that when happiness disappears, people are choosing "between a mere philosophical speculation and the clear testimony of the Bible...."[8]

Those who fall between mere philosophical speculation and the Bible are those who speculate about what God's love really *is or isn't* rather than relying upon what God tells us in His Word. One of the great speculations is that God had originated the evil that has now befallen them. There are indeed some Christians who firmly believe that God created everything—including evil. Because of this belief, we may hear Christians say, when stricken with cancer, "Why did God give this to me? I thought He loved me." I've heard many women who say, after their husband has left them, "I know this divorce is God's will for my life." Of course, they might say this because they want to glorify God in their situation. But really, is divorce God's will? In light of Malachi 2:16, where God said, "I hate divorce," I don't think so. We need to recognize that God is good and does good (Psalm 119:68).

We have to be careful about trying to figure out explanations for the bad things that occur to us. Yes, divorce, a friend's betrayal, or even cancer may be permitted by God, but that doesn't mean they originated from Him. All His works and ways are utterly opposed to all evil. He is not darkness, but light (John 8:12); not evil, but love. Just as God cautions men against judging one another on the basis of appearances, so much more must we be careful about making the mistake in judging Him, "for He does not afflict willingly, or grieve the sons of men" (Lamentations 3:33).

> God wants us to get to the end of ourselves, to wean us away from earthly things, and to fix our hearts on the eternal.

When bad situations come our way, we need to make a distinction between God's perfect will (us living in obedience) and God's permissive will (sin occurred, such as a husband leaving), and recognize that ultimately, God can work through the bad and bear good from it (Romans 8:28).

God's love is not a cold and ineffectual love that consists only in raw wishes. Rather, it's an active love that works to accomplish what He intends to do with us. For instance, sometimes He permits us to sink just as Peter did when he took his eyes off Christ while walking on water (Matthew 14:28-30). God wants us to get to the end of ourselves, to wean us away from earthly things, and to fix our hearts on the eternal.

Consider the people of Moab. God said they had never been through any purifying trials to remove the bitterness from their lives—"therefore he retains his flavor, and his aroma has not changed" (Jeremiah 48:11). A life without problems is an unrefined life, which would leave our scent unchanged. Because of this, there could never be a sweet aroma coming from our life. Instead, we would continually stink. Therefore, we can be thankful when problems come along. Pain and suffering provide us with opportunities to become more compassionate and generous toward others. Who can calculate the extent to which your life will affect another for the good, because of your difficult experiences? Thankfully, we have available the provision of Christ's love for us. He will, as He has in the past, help us cope with the trials in a world that has no place for Him. And one day, our mourning will end.

The Promise of Comfort

There is a promise from God that is a source of comfort when we are going through sorrow and pain: "The days of your mourning will be finished" (Isaiah 60:20). If you are currently suffering, your mourning will end, and you will have changed for the better because of it. Let's go down Scripture's memory lane and see what happened to some individuals who suffered, and note what the turnout was.

Remember when Jacob was feeling grief, believing all things were against him? Remember when he thought his sons Joseph and Simeon were dead (Genesis 42:36)? Well, God's promise came through. Jacob's mourning ended when he learned his sons weren't dead. God took the trial of grief and Jacob became "revived" (Genesis 45:26).

Who can forget what poor Elijah went through at the hands of his enemies? He was afraid and depressed beyond measure. He even asked God to take his life (1 Kings 19:4). His mourning came to an end when God sent an angel to feed him and give him strength (1 Kings 19:7-8).

God took the trial of fear and depression and enabled Elijah to be able to go on with life (1 Kings 19:5-8).

What parent wouldn't feel compassion for the grieving Shunammite woman who found her son dead? She tried ever so hard to hold on to her faith, but her soul had become troubled within her (2 Kings 4:20,27). Her mourning came to an end when Elisha brought her son back to life. Here, God took the trials of grief and a troubled soul, and turned them into an overwhelming sense of gratitude (2 Kings 4:37). Then there were the Jewish people, who were in captivity, agony, and being humiliated by those who were at ease (Psalm 123:3-4). God ended their mourning by delivering them from the hands of their enemies and restoring them. He took their trial of captivity and gave them reason to have great joy.

Psalm 126:5-6 tells us, "Those who sow in tears shall reap with joyful shouting. He who goes to and fro weeping, carrying his bag of seed, shall indeed come again with a shout of joy, bringing his sheaves with him." It's been said that you must cut a diamond to see its value and bring out the fullness of its colors under a light. Afflictions bring to light what is in the heart. Those who know God's love and are eternally grateful for what He did for them (1 Peter 2:24) show off their colors by exhibiting strong faith, profound gratitude, and energetic spiritual power. And these are manifest best *not* when life is going well for them, but when they've gone through the dark night of struggle. Knowing that God will "wipe tears away from all faces" (Isaiah 25:8), we can, even in our greatest suffering and our most troubling trials, witness to others the most glorious truth that "God is love" (1 John 4:7-8).

Key Truths about God's Love

Some women feel so awful over their past sin that despite their repentance and God's loving forgiveness, they feel they can never be as close to the Lord again. One woman shared, after her adulterous affair, "God will never see me as lovely ever again."

If you feel this way, keep in mind that God looks at your whole heart, and not just your past sin. Your sin may be all you can see when you look at your life, but God sees your *whole* life, and not just where your heart gave way to sin.

He Looks at the Heart

Sin in David's heart resulted in his share of failings—some of which permanently branded him. For example, who hasn't heard about his adulterous affair with Bathsheba? Or about his plot to have her husband, Uriah, killed in a battle?

Despite David being branded, God, who knew David's heart perfectly, said of him *after the sin was committed* that David was a man who "kept My commandments and who followed Me with all his heart, to do only that which was right in My sight" (1 Kings 14:8).

What a marvelous statement! What divine love shown! If we sinned the way David did, we would probably feel as though that's all God would remember about our lives.

Look, too, at Asa. A prophet told him that he had acted foolishly by relying on the king of Syria rather than upon God. He rebuked Asa, saying, "You have acted foolishly in this. Indeed, from now on you will surely have wars" (2 Chronicles 16:9). Asa preferred not to listen to the messenger, who also said, "The eyes of the LORD move to and fro throughout the earth that He may strongly support those whose heart is completely His" (verse 9). Rather than think about God protecting those whose hearts are completely His, Asa threw the messenger in prison (2 Chronicles 16:10). And yet despite such outrageous behavior, it was said of Asa that his "heart was blameless all his days" (2 Chronicles 15:17).

What about the woman caught in adultery in John chapter 8? The scribes and Pharisees wanted to have her stoned. Imagine her fighting against those men, trying to defend herself as they call her horrible names and throw her down on the hard ground. Observe her rolling up into a ball, covering her head from the stones that would surely be thrown at her in anger. This was the scenario when Jesus came to the rescue.

The accusers were trying to justify, before Jesus, their actions against the woman. But the Lord knew what they were really trying to do. They wanted to trap Jesus and accuse Him of not upholding the law (John 8:6).

Ignoring the religious leaders, "Jesus stooped down and with His finger wrote on the ground" (John 8:6). What He wrote, we aren't told. But we do know what He did next. He said to the accusers, "He who is without sin among you, let him be the first to throw a stone at her" (John 8:7).

At first, there was silence. Then, one by one, the accusers slowly walked away. Now the woman was left alone with Jesus, and by now her humiliation was known to the entire community.

Now comes the best part of the story: the conversation between Jesus and this nameless woman. We first notice that Jesus called her "woman" (John 8:10). You may say, "Well, so did the scribes and Pharisees" (see John 8:4). Yes, you are right, but there's a difference here. The Greek word for woman is *guné,* which is used as a term of respect and endearment."[9] From that comes *gunaikarion,* which can mean either "a little woman," or contemptuously, a "silly woman, a poor weak woman."[10] We can be sure the Pharisees and scribes used the term in a condescending way—saying that she was silly or weak. The way they had treated her, they couldn't have been referring to her as a woman in a respectful way.

Jesus, however, *did* call her "woman" in the respectful sense—just as He had done so with His mother (John 19:26). After the woman caught in adultery had received such horrible treatment from the Pharisees and scribes, imagine how she must have felt. What love Jesus was bestowing upon her!

Rather than give this hurting woman a stern lecture regarding her sin, He asked, "Woman, where are they? Did no one condemn you?" (John 8:10).

"No one, Lord," she replied.

"Neither do I condemn you," Jesus said. Then He added, "Go. From now on sin no more" (verse 11).

How refreshing this must have been to a woman who felt like she couldn't be accepted or loved by anyone. In the midst of all her trouble, she now knew that someone genuinely loved her.

If we have a hard time believing Jesus can love us even after we sin, we need to remember that *we are objects of His lovingkindness.* He's zealous for us with a fervent love that never ends, "I have loved you with an everlasting love" (Jeremiah 31:3). It's a love that has "drawn you with lovingkindness" (Jeremiah 31:3). This love is loyal and steadfast. It's a love that stresses a belonging together: "I will betroth you to Me forever" (Hosea 2:19). God's love is faithful, and nothing we could ever do will take away that love.

He Cares for You

We are exhorted in Scripture to "*behold* what manner of love the Father hath bestowed upon us" (1 John 3:1 KJV). The word "behold" implies complete amazement in His love. It brings to our attention the kind of love the Lord shows to us—the "manner of love."

For example, Jesus observes a despised and very lonely Zaccheus up in a sycamore tree. As a Jewish tax gatherer working for the hated Romans, Zaccheus had no friends. The Jews disliked him because he worked for the Romans, and the Romans hated him because he was a Jew. But Jesus showed Zaccheus respect. With Jesus' one little act, divine love conquered the tax collector's heart, and Zaccheus proclaimed, "Behold, Lord, half of my possessions I will give to the poor, and if I have defrauded anyone of anything, I will give back four times as much" (Luke 19:8).

Elsewhere, we see Jesus talking to a broken man—a man who had denied Him—and Jesus invites the man back into the same relationship they had before the denial. Jesus asked Peter, "Do you love me?" (John 21:15-17), and love changed him from a reluctant betrayer into a willing martyr (John 21:18).

Jesus' love for a sinful woman led her to anoint His feet with costly perfume (Luke 7:44-46). And His compassion on an afflicted woman led Him to call her "daughter" (Mark 5:34), heal her body and soul, and take away her fear and replace it with peace (Mark 5:32-34).

Just as Jesus had a tender love for the erring Peter (John 21:15-25) and doubting Thomas (John 20:25-28), He has a tender love for you and has forgiven you of your sins. He who had a protective heart for His disciples and warned, "See to it that no one misleads you" (Matthew 24:4) has a protective heart for you. He who accepted the rejected children and said, "The kingdom

> We are His bride, and as such, He thinks about us, plans for us, watches over us.

of heaven belongs to such as these" (Matthew 19:13-15) has accepted you. Just as He took special care of the blind and the deaf, the lame and the diseased, He takes special care of you. Just as He mixed His tears with the sobs of those by the grave of Lazarus (John 11:33-34), He mixes His tears with yours. What love!

You Are Precious to God

We live in the hearts of those who love us. And it's clear that we live in the heart of Jesus. We are His bride, and as such, He thinks about us, plans for us, watches over us. Our sorrows, pain, and distresses are felt by Him as if they were His own. He prays for us: "I pray for them" (John 17:9 KJV); "I ask on their behalf" (John 17:9). And He talks to the Father about us: "Holy Father, keep them in Your name...that they may be one even as We are" (John 17:11).

If you feel as though Jesus loves you less than others, please think again. He has put you into the same relationship, under the same care, and into the same place in His heart as His disciples! Just as He told them, He tells you: "I will send [the Helper, the Holy Spirit] to you" (John 16:7); "Because I live, you will live also" (John 14:19); and "I go and prepare a place for you, I will come again and receive you to Myself, that where I am, there you may be also" (John 14:3). He is passionate about you, as His Word reveals: "I will betroth you to Me forever" (Hosea 2:19); and "It will come about in that day…that you will call Me Ishi [husband]" (Hosea 2:16).[11]

We are to be excited about His love, passionate about our relationship with Him. We are to be thankful that His yearning heart has put us in the marriage-covenant we have with Him. We are to tell others about His love just as a bride talks about her groom's love for her. We see His love for us in these words: "You are precious in My sight…you are honored and I love you" (Isaiah 43:4), so "Come" (Revelation 22:17), the marriage banquet is ready!

The Marriage Banquet

All things are now ready, oh, please come!
Celebrate in My love; observe what I have done.

I prepared a marriage banquet, for you, My bride,
Sit down at My table, be at My side.

Take of the spread, of My fullness of grace.
Enjoy every morsel, as we sit face to face.

For you My bride, for this moment I died.
I now give you My Name, wear it with pride.

Impossible it is, for there to be night,
So true is My love—out of sight.

Forever I'll love you, forever, I say
Never, oh never shall it fade away.[12]

—D.M.

Our Passion in Action

1. Are there any hindrances that have kept you from receiving God's love for you? What action do you need to take to remove the hindrance(s)?

2. Do you have a special story you would like to share with a friend or your Bible study group about God's love toward you?

3. Start a testimony of love. Get a journal and begin recording each time you notice God's revealing love for you. When you feel low, you will be able to refer back to the journal and be encouraged and reminded of His love.

4. To begin reminding yourself throughout the day of God's love for you, write down one or more of the following verses found in note 13 on page 235. Tape your chosen verse(s) up throughout the house where you can see them often—on the refrigerator, above the washer and dryer, behind the kitchen cupboard, doors, etc. Read and meditate upon these verses whenever you see them.

PART 2:

Building Your
Passion for Jesus

5

Living Out Your Marriage Vow to Christ

"For You have heard my vows....
So I will sing praise to Your name forever,
that I may pay my vows day by day."
—PSALM 61:8

In 1834, Samuel Parker, a persuasive Congregational pastor, traveled by horseback throughout western New York proclaiming a compelling message about the need to spread the gospel in a God-forsaken land called Oregon. He told about the Indians who lived there and how hungry they were for God's truth.

Listening to Parker in the village of Wheeler was Marcus Whitman, a 32-year-old doctor who zealously wanted to share Christ with the Native Americans Parker spoke about. In another town, called Amity, Narcissa Prentiss also heard Parker. She was an unusually gifted woman. The daughter of an eminent judge, she was well educated and attractive. At age 26 she had not yet married, which puzzled many. In her day, if a woman wasn't married by that age, she was called a spinster.

Narcissa committed her life to Jesus at the young age of 11. By the time she was 16 she desired to become a missionary and share Christ with the lost. So when she heard Dr. Parker's plea for missionaries, she thought his message was an answer to her prayers. She signed up immediately. There was only one problem: Dr. Parker's mission board refused Narcissa because she was single. Her only chance at becoming a missionary was to find a husband with the same burning zeal to go west. He would also have to have qualifications just as exceptional as hers.

Dr. Parker came up with a solution—a great one, so he thought. He hooked Narcissa up with Marcus Whitman. The mission board, however, questioned Marcus. Back then, a doctor of medicine didn't have as high a status as a doctor of divinity. So even though Narcissa would have her problem solved, Marcus wouldn't have his solved. Marcus decided to prove himself to the mission board by taking an exploratory trip to the western side of the Rockies—alone. He told everyone, including Narcissa, that he would be gone for a full year. Narcissa protested, but her pleas didn't do any good. Marcus went out anyway. After being gone for a while, Marcus got lonely and returned home so he could marry Narcissa. Upon their engagement, the missionary board decided they would accept both Marcus and Narcissa as missionaries—under the condition that another couple accompany them.

And so, as the story goes, Marcus and Narcissa were married in a Presbyterian church in February 1836. This was about two years after first hearing Dr. Parker's stirring missionary call.

The wedding was unlike a traditional one. All Narcissa's relatives, including the females, were in black. Narcissa herself had chosen to wear a black wedding dress. Why, we do not know. Perhaps money was tight, and she did not want to spend it on an expensive, luxurious dress when she would be spending the rest of her life out in the rugged Oregon Territory.

Throughout the entire ceremony people could be heard crying, most assuredly, out of joy. But then came the real tear jerker when Narcissa sang the song "Missionary Farewell."

Yes, my native land I love thee
All thy scenes I love them well;
Friends, connections, happy country,
Can I bid you all farewell?
Can I leave you, Can I leave you
Far in heathen lands to dwell?[1]

We can see here that Narcissa was indeed ready to forsake all for Jesus. And later on, she would die as a martyr (another story for another time). But what makes this story turn from joy to discomfort—or at least awkwardness—is that the following day, as Narcissa and Marcus began their honeymoon, the other couple accompanied them. At first glance, that might not seem so bad. But the mission board assigned the newlyweds to go out with Henry and Eliza Spaulding. Henry had at one time declared his love to Narcissa and proposed marriage to her. *And so the plot thickens.*

Even though time had passed and Narcissa was now married to Marcus, Henry was still smoldering with resentment. He still had deep emotions for Narcissa. So we can imagine how awkward this setup was!

This went on for a while, for Henry and Narcissa ministered side by side, lived tent by tent, and prayed together. I don't know about you, but I couldn't do that! Yes, I am a sister in Christ with some men I dated long ago, but I wouldn't want them to accompany me on my honeymoon! Nor would I feel comfortable ministering with them side by side.

How difficult it must have been for Narcissa to live out her marriage vow in the presence of another man who had wanted to marry her! Most assuredly, Narcissa and her husband felt they needed to make the best of the situation, for the sake of those who needed Jesus.

Now, let's take a look at ourselves, the bride of Christ. Are there any circumstances that hinder us as we pursue our relationship with Jesus? Is there anyone or anything in our life that is hindering a full devotion to Jesus? Is something getting in the way of our marriage vow to Him?

What distractions keep us from living a life full of spiritual passion for Him? There are many hindrances that can get in the way, and one of the more common ones is living a halfhearted, shallow Christian life. In other words, a *lukewarm* life. It's that awful word—lukewarmness.

Defining Spiritual Lukewarmness

In Revelation 3:1, Jesus said, "I know your deeds, that you have a name that you are alive, but you are dead." While Jesus here is speaking of churchgoers who are actually nonbelievers, it's still good for us to evaluate ourselves. He later added, "Because you are lukewarm, and neither hot nor cold, I will spit you out of My mouth" (Revelation 3:16).

What type of heart do we have?

The hot, passionate, on-fire heart can't get enough of Jesus. Those who are spiritually passionate like the Emmaus disciples who said after talking to Jesus, "Were not our hearts burning within us while He was speaking to us?" (Luke 24:32).

The cold heart doesn't have Jesus at all. It appears that there are two varieties of coldness. One type of cold heart is open to the things of the Lord for a while. But for one reason or another, the heart grows cold (Matthew 24:12). This type of person was never saved, for Matthew 24:13 says, "He who *endures to the end* will be saved." This verse doesn't suggest that our perseverance secures our salvation, for true believers "are protected by the power of God through faith for salvation" (1 Peter 1:5). Rather, those who are truly saved will not depart from the Lord (Jeremiah 32:40). And those who do fall away from Christ give proof they were never truly followers of Jesus (1 John 2:19).[2]

The other type of cold heart never shows any interest toward Jesus. I once shared about Christ to a woman who thought that belief in Jesus was "what children's make-believe stories are made of."

The lukewarm heart is fickle—who knows if it has Jesus or not? In the original Greek text, the word "lukewarm" is *chliaros*. This means the condition of the soul wretchedly fluctuates between a passive and a fervent love.[3] I'm sure we've all been passive from time to time, and fervent other times. But if our heart stays consistently lukewarm, then we must be warned: "Because you are lukewarm...I will spit you out of My mouth" (Revelation 3:16).

Why is Christ so repulsed by a lukewarm heart? Because such a person—who calls himself a Christian—is obstructing the progress of true spiritual Christianity in the world. How? By acting too much like the world in his actions, words, and deeds—leaving Jesus out of the picture.

Prior to my friend Mary becoming a Christian, she used to tell me how turned off she was by a co-worker who called himself a born-again believer but behaved horribly. I told Mary she couldn't judge all believers by this one individual. She agreed, but one day Mary finally exclaimed, "That guy is really turning me off to Christianity!"

Mary's disgust prompted me to evaluate my life. I realized I can't attract others to Christ if I am not glorifying the Lord in all I say and do. Others are watching me, and they are watching you, too.

Examining Our Life

Are you willing to examine your life? Below is a checklist of 11 ways to tell whether lukewarmness might have crept into our life. Lord willing, you won't find anything on this list that describes you. But if so, be honest with yourself...and get rid of whatever hinders you.

1. *We pursue earthly riches more than spiritual riches.* Are we thinking about that big-screen TV, a new car, that luxurious vacation more than about what really matters? Do we complain because we don't have everything we want? Is our heart focused more on the things of earth or the things of the Spirit?

Consider the Laodicean people. They were churchgoers, and most likely nice people. They were also wealthy and lived in a lovely area. Life seemed quite good to them. But Jesus rebuked them, saying, "You do not know that you are wretched and miserable and poor and blind and naked" (Revelation 3:17). While they were materially rich, they were also spiritually poor. Now, there are many wealthy people in Scripture that God blessed and never rebuked. So wealth wasn't the issue, but the people's hearts. They had "set their minds on earthly things" (Philippians 3:19). They had gratified their earthly desires and had come to believe they had "need of nothing" (Revelation 3:17). Jesus suggested to them, "Buy from Me gold refined by fire" (Revelation 3:18). In other words, it's the spiritual riches that matter.

2. *We know we aren't right with God, but we aren't correcting ourselves.* As Christians we are called to obedience. As Scripture says, "Return, O faithless sons...for I am a master to you" (Jeremiah 3:14). If we don't desire to turn from our backsliding ways and obey Jesus, then we neither love or have Him. Nor are we married to Him. Jesus asks, "Why do you call Me, 'Lord, Lord,' and do not do what I say?" (Luke 6:46). To know God and love Him is to obey Him (John 14:15,21). How do we get into the practice of complete obedience? Peter tells us how: "Gird up the loins of your mind" (1 Peter 1:13 NKJV). Back in Peter's day, people wore long garments they would gird up so the clothing wouldn't interfere with their activities. So Peter is telling us to gird up our mind: control our thoughts and reject all hindrances that would cause us to disobey. Peter then said, "As He who called you is holy, you also be holy in all your conduct, because it is written, 'Be holy, for I am holy'" (1 Peter 1:15-16 NKJV).

> True ministry is *never* convenient, but it is *always* compassionate.

3. *We aren't seeking God's will for our life.* I once talked with a woman who was taking some questionable steps in her life and asked her why she was convinced she was following God's will. She said, "Because I'm happy. Doesn't God want me happy?" What she was doing was assuming that

her will was God's will. We need to make sure we haven't placed our selfish desires over and above God's desires. That's why Jesus taught the disciples to seek and pray for God's will (Matthew 6:10). His will is always best for our lives. A vibrant, zealous, passionate Christian will not rest until she knows God's will for her.

4. *We are hesitant to help others.* Sometimes no matter how much we would like to help someone, our circumstances don't allow us. But what about those times when we give excuses to get out of helping a person who asks for assistance? Are we serving only when it's "convenient"? True ministry is *never* convenient, but it is *always* compassionate. Helping others is always a result of compassion. And who are we to be compassionate toward? First, *to other believers.* We are to "have the same care for one another" (1 Corinthians 12:25). We are also to be compassionate *toward those who are afflicted:* "For the despairing man there should be kindness from his friend; so that he does not forsake the fear of the Almighty" (Job 6:14). *For the chastened* who need our help, despite the fact they may not come to ask for it: "Therefore I say, 'Turn your eyes away from me, let me weep bitterly, do not try to comfort me…'" (Isaiah 22:4). *For the poor:* "One who is gracious to a poor man lends to the LORD, and He will repay him for his good deed" (Proverbs 19:17). *For the weak:* "Bear one another's burdens" (Galatians 6:2). And even *for our enemies:* "But I say to you, love your enemies" (Matthew 5:44); "bless those who persecute you" (Romans 12:14); "not returning evil for evil or insult for insult, but giving a blessing instead" (1 Peter 3:9). "So then, while we have opportunity, let us do good *to all people*" (Galatians 6:10). And as we do good for others, let's be challenged by Paul's exhortation to be "not lagging behind in diligence, fervent in spirit, serving the Lord" (Romans 12:11).

5. *We do not live our life to the glory of God.* Some Christians are confused as to what it means to glorify God. This is an overused phrase that can easily lose its meaning. Glorifying God is magnifying who He is—

not only in our words, but also by imitating Him in our deeds. Glorifying Him means putting God's goodness on display in our lives, *showing the world what He is like.*

Unfortunately, we can easily sing "To God Be the Glory" in church one day, then the following day be gossiping about a sister in Christ. Paul noticed this phenomenon as well. He said that our tongues are "full of deadly poison" (James 3:8) and "with it we bless our Lord and Father, and with it we curse men, who have been made in the likeness of God; from the same mouth come both blessing and cursing" (James 3:9-10). Paul said, "My brethren, these things ought not to be this way" (James 3:10). The passionate woman is sensitive about her walk with Jesus and desires to honor and please Him in all her ways—in what she thinks, what she does, and what she says. She wants to hide herself in Christ. In other words, she wants others to see Jesus in her, to know who He is through her godly life.

6. *We aren't thinking about growing spiritually.* Because you are reading this book, I know you are indeed concerned about your spiritual growth. But how easily we can slip into the routines of everyday life and forget about our spiritual life. To keep that from happening, we need to be on our knees in frequent and humble prayer before God. We need to ask Him to let us know how we need to change, to help us transform a weakness or further develop a strength. We need to have a plan for consistent spiritual growth to ensure ourselves that *we will* be different six months from now.

7. *We have made a profession of Christ, but still doubt our salvation.* We can truly know of our salvation if we are trusting in Jesus alone for it (John 14:6), and not our "works" (Ephesians 2:8-9). As well, we know we are a Christian if we are living out the fruit of the Spirit: "love, joy, peace, patience, kindness, goodness, faithfulness, gentleness, self-control" (Galatians 5:22-23) and have "crucified the flesh with its passions and desires" (Galatians 5:24). Another way to know is if we are living and

walking by the Spirit of God (Galatians 5:25). If you are still unsure of your salvation, turn to "Do You Belong to Jesus?" on page 227.

8. *We neglect to read God's Word on a regular basis.* When we get out of the habit of being in God's Word, we are no longer concerned with what He has to say to us. Jesus' wonderful Word (which we'll talk about in greater depth in chapter 9) feeds us and builds us up. Our heart and life are like a garden. If we leave them alone, they will be barren or over-grown with weeds. They *must* be tilled, sown, and cared for.

9. *We aren't in the habit of daily prayer.* The purpose of prayer isn't to tell God what He doesn't already know or to dictate or suggest to Him what to do or what to give us. Prayer keeps us *clinging* to Jesus. In prayer we confess to Him that we do know and feel our own needs, and that we acknowledge He alone can supply our needs. To pray is to submit to His timing for the answer and His decision as to how to answer. As we come to Him in prayer, He will fight our battles; He will allow us to conquer in every struggle with evil. It's a fact the spiritually passionate woman walks where angels fear to tread—with good reason, she needs to pray: to conquer and to grow spiritually. While we'll talk about prayer later in this book, we can sum it up here by saying that when we live the same day after day, without relying upon God and His Word and going to Him in prayer, we are in danger of becoming lukewarm and acting from bad habits rather than from a conscious desire to work on our relationship with Jesus. Remember what God said to the Israelites? "Can a virgin forget her ornaments, or a bride her attire? Yet My people have forgotten Me days without number" (Jeremiah 2:32). Have we been forgetting Jesus?

10. *Others don't know we belong to Jesus.* How many people know you are a follower of the Lord Jesus Christ? How many know that Jesus comes first in your life before all else? How many know that you refuse to compromise your faith?

If few know of your commitment to Jesus, it's possible you never made a true commitment. Or if people cannot see any difference between your lifestyle and that of the world, then it would be best for you to "test yourselves to see if you are in the faith; examine yourselves!" (2 Corinthians 13:5). Jesus said that if we haven't picked up our cross and followed Him, then we aren't worthy of Him (Matthew 10:38).

11. *We are attending a lukewarm church.* In Scripture we see Christ is knocking on the door of the Laodicean church (Revelation 3:20). He is outside rather than inside, and thus the church is lukewarm (Revelation 3:16).

What does a lukewarm church look like? It has the appearance of the secular rather than of the spiritual. Leaders are chosen according to secular career and position rather than spiritual maturity and passion. Wealth and status are recognized and spiritual growth is not. Rising church membership is a greater concern than the presence of the Spirit. Spiritual zeal is considered odd instead of normal. And the people have become "dull of hearing" (Hebrews 5:11).

We may wonder, *Why would Christ want to enter such a church?* Because His hope is that He can spiritually revive some of those members. "Those whom I love, I reprove and discipline; be zealous therefore, and *repent*" (Revelation 3:19). But until that church opens its door to Him, the people will stay spiritually impoverished.

Avoiding Spiritual Lukewarmness

If you fear that you may have become lukewarm and want to change, you can. The first step, as Jesus shows us, is to "repent" (Revelation 3:19). Next, get into the habit of praying and reading God's Word daily. These are the means of obtaining likeness to God. Prayer and Scripture also help us to "be transformed by the renewing of your mind" (Romans 12:2). Interestingly, the Greek word for "transformed," *metamorphoō*,[4] is the same word used to describe the transfiguration of Christ before

Peter, James, and John (Matthew 17:2; Mark 9:2)—when He changed in appearance and "became white and gleaming" (Luke 9:29). Prayer and the Word are what transform us so we reflect Christlikeness here on earth. And someday, "when He appears, we shall be like Him, because we shall see Him just as He is" (1 John 3:2).

When we renew our minds, we drive out the likeness of the world from us. We become Christlike, desiring Jesus more and the world less. We think more about our soul and less about our body. We think more about eternity and less about this world. We are more concerned about what God thinks of us and less about what others think.

Another way to avoid becoming lukewarm is to be around others who are passionate for Jesus. As the saying goes, "If you want to stay warm, you've got to keep near the fire." Where do you find these passionate people? In passionate churches. Paul the apostle showed such passion in the Corinthian church that he proclaimed, "You are in our hearts to die together and to live together" (2 Corinthians 7:3). While this verse may sound poetic, these words aren't just beautiful prose. Paul is telling us we should be in fellowship with other believers such that our hearts are united in purpose as we live and die together in Christ—as we "encourage one another and build up one another" (1 Thessalonians 5:11).

Is the church you are currently attending lukewarm, keeping Jesus outside? If so, and attempts at change seem futile, then you may need to search for a church that passionately preaches Christ and His Word; a church that is humbly at the foot of the cross and stays there; a church that is concerned about your spiritual well-being. You will find spiritually passionate people there. And if you live too great a distance from such a church, you can try to find a respected Bible teacher with either a radio or tape ministry and make that teaching your avenue of spiritual growth. Of course, a key part of your spiritual growth will be digging into the Word yourself and asking the Spirit of God to guide you in understanding it.

As you think about the condition of your current church, ask the Lord how *you* might be of help in bringing about change. Perhaps you could begin some sort of ministry in your church—a women's Bible study or prayer group, or some other means that allows you to offer the surpassing riches of Jesus Christ (Ephesians 2:7) to other women. And before you take such steps, pray fervently that the Lord will first of all revive your soul—"revive me according to Your lovingkindness" (Psalm 119:88). If you are lacking for the right words to say, you might find the following prayer helpful. It was written by a Puritan in the 1600s who was mournful over his lack of spiritual passion.

> If thy mercy had bounds, where would be my refuge from
>   just wrath?
> But thy love in Christ is without measure.
> Thus, I present myself to thee
>   with sins of commission and omission,
>   against thee, my Father,
>   against thee, adorable redeemer,
>   against thee and thy strivings, O Holy Spirit,
>   against the dictates of my conscience,
>   against the precepts of thy Word,
>   against my neighbours and myself.
> Enter not into judgment with me,
> For I plead no righteousness of my own,
>   and have no cloak for iniquity.
> Pardon my day dark with evil.
> This night I renew my penitence.
> Every morning I vow to love thee more fervently,
>   to serve thee more sincerely
>   to be more devoted in my life,
>   to be wholly thine;
> Yet I soon stumble, backslide,
>   and have to confess my weakness, misery and sin.

But I bless thee that the finished work of Jesus needs no
    addition
            from my doings,
            that his oblation is sufficient satisfaction
            for my sins.
If future days be mine, help me to amend my life,
            to hate evil and abhor evil,
            to flee the sins I confess.
Make me more resolute, more watchful, more prayerful.
Let no evil fruit spring from evil seeds my hands have
    sown;
Let no neighbour be hardened in vanity and folly
    by my want of circumspection.
If this day I have been ashamed of Christ and his Word,
    or have shown unkindness, malice, envy, lack of love,
    unadvised speech, hasty temper,
    let it be no stumbling block to others,
    or dishonor to thy name.
O help me to set an upright example
    that will ever rebuke vice,
    allure to goodness,
    and evidence
    that lovely are the ways of Christ.[5]

Yes, *lovely are the ways of Christ* as we strive onward and upward in our spiritual growth—from our new birth, to our infancy, to our youth, and most of all, to our spiritual maturity. Such a beautiful life is maintained by Jesus, faith, the Word of God, and prayer. And as we grow, we become more and more passionate about our vows to Jesus: "You have heard my vows.... So I will sing praise to Your name forever, that I may pay my vows day by day" (Psalm 61:5,8). What vows might these be? They can be a variety of vows that we make to Jesus. But there is one special vow that I believe best describes our life with Jesus.

Reliving Our Vow to Jesus

The woman of spiritual passion is like a bride who is ever zealous for her groom, and rightly so. For who in heaven or on earth can compare with our heavenly Groom, Jesus? Who is more precious? Who can compare with His wisdom? Who else can prepare for us a home in heaven? And while He prepares a heavenly place for us, He is the greatest provider any bride could ask for here on earth. In Galatians 2:20, the apostle Paul wrote some words that could, in essence, be our wedding vow—a vow we can live by "day by day" (Psalm 61:8), a vow that can control our entire spiritual life:

> Our lifetime wedding vow to Jesus is to be crucified with Him.

I have been crucified with Christ;
and it is no longer I who live, but Christ lives in me;
and the life which I now live in the flesh
I live by faith in the Son of God,
who loved me and gave Himself up for me.

Crucified with Him

Our lifetime wedding vow to Jesus is to be crucified with Him. As the bride of Christ, we've made a lifetime commitment that sets self aside and yields our all to Jesus. We are crucifying our soul, our will, our thoughts, our heart, and most of all, our flesh. This means dying to worldliness and laying our plans of happiness at the altar. Self dies hard, so we must frequently ask ourselves, "Have I really died?"

What is it about the crucified life that scares away many but attracts others? Well, I can't answer for everyone, but I know that for me, I am attracted to the fact that I am being crucified not just on any cross, but upon Jesus' cross—the cross that took Him back to the Father. It's a cross that not only lifts up the fallen, but as we are raised, it's a cross that helps us live the spiritual life. It begins with humility and obedience (Philippians 2:8). What woman wants that? Certainly not a worldly woman, for it goes completely against the modern feminist message and contemporary society's values. Only the person who is spiritually passionate would consider it. The spiritually passionate woman embraces the cross of Jesus and empties herself of her pride and her own desires as she takes on "the form of a bond-servant" (Philippians 2:7), surrendering herself to God and others. And as she surrenders to God, she desires to be obedient to Him, extending herself to the will of God in every part of her life until the day of her death.

Because Christ lives in her, she has an earnest desire to crucify her soul, her will, her thoughts, her heart, and most of all, her flesh. She lays at the altar her plans of happiness, and says first, "Thy will be done" (Matthew 6:10) before she asks, "Give us this day our daily bread" (Matthew 6:11). Jesus lives in her, His Spirit guides her, and the Father is glorified through her. What bliss this is for her! Certainly, to the perishing, it is foolishness (1 Corinthians 1:18), but for her it is wonderful because as she dies to self, she is living in Christ.

If you aren't sure whether you have truly been crucified with Christ, all you need to do is evaluate whether you have really died to the things of this world. Can you say with Paul, "It is no longer I who live"?

We have died when we live by the motto "If Christ is *my* sacrifice, then *I* am His." This entails our willingness to go through whatever sacrifice God wills for us. This is what it means to live in "the fellowship of His sufferings" (Philippians 3:10), be "conformed to His death" (Philippians 3:10), become like Him in His death. And what was He like in death? He was selfless; He was concerned about the salvation of others; He cared not for His own comforts. Rather, He cared for our comforts and eternal well-being.

As we become like Jesus in death, we must expect to go through what He went through. Jesus said, "If they persecuted Me, they will also persecute you" (John 15:20). *Externally* we will suffer because of the evil around us, because of those who hate Jesus, because of those who have a hard time being around us as we reflect the Light of this world. *Internally* we will struggle against the temptations of this world, the mean actions of others, the outside influences that can affect our thinking. The conflict can indeed be difficult and painful, but we can fight against it. How do we do that? By living by faith. Let's take a closer look....

Faith in Him

While Paul still lived in the flesh, he no longer had confidence in it (Philippians 3:4-8). His ruling power was "faith in the Son of God" (Galatians 2:20). Everyone has faith. And what is faith? It's trust. Yet the faith of a Christian is different from the faith of those in the world. The woman of the world has faith in either herself (and her good works) or in her possessions—or both. The woman of spiritual passion has faith *only* in Jesus Christ—a faith that enables her to trust in God's power rather than her own understanding (Proverbs 3:5-6). She especially trusts Him when she faces the difficulties in "the valley," "the river," "the shadow," and "the unknown."

Unquestioning faith knows God will never ask us to do anything without good reason. If we have unquestioning faith, we will be abundantly blessed. If we have a reserving faith, then our blessings will be limited by our capacity to receive. A strong, vibrant faith believes there is no limit to God's love and His power to bless. He gives in overflowing measure, far beyond our expectations, far beyond what we deserve. But we may stifle the blessing for ourselves and others. We see examples in Scripture of people whose lack of faith hindered the possibility of larger spiritual blessing. Elisha was displeased with King Joash (also known as Jehoash) because of what he viewed was a lack of faith. Elisha told the king to take the Lord's arrow of victory and strike it to the ground to defeat the Arameans. King Joash did as Elisha requested but struck the ground only three times and stopped (2 Kings 13:18). Elisha rebuked Joash, telling him, "You should have struck five or six times, then you would have struck Aram until you would have destroyed it. But now you shall strike Aram only three times" (2 Kings 13:19). Joash's blessing was not as abundant as it could have been.

When our faith is strong, it grows and we are given greater spiritual blessing. "For whoever has, to him more shall be given" (Mark 4:25). Yet when our faith is weak, we are hindered in our growth. We can also forfeit blessing by neglecting our faith or by harboring sin in our hearts: "If I regard iniquity in my heart, the Lord will not hear" (Psalm 66:18).

Thankfully, as we stay in a right relationship with the Lord, He will hear us (Psalm 66:19-20). More than that, we are given this promise: "He who overcomes, I will grant to him to sit down with Me on My throne…" (Revelation 3:21). Can you even conceive of the great joy and bliss you will experience when you first see Jesus? Imagine—it all started with Jesus' crucified life and your identity with it when you vowed, "It is no longer I who live, but Christ lives in me" (Galatians 2:20). Indeed, "I will sing praise to Your name forever, that I may pay my vows day by day" (Psalm 61:8).

Wonderfully, our vow of the crucified life not only helps us live the spiritual life here on earth, but it also makes us ready to be received by Jesus when He calls us home.

> Let us rejoice and be glad and
> give the glory to Him,
> for the marriage of the Lamb has come and
> His bride has made herself ready.
> —Revelation 19:7

Your Passion in Action

1. What are some of the reasons people become lukewarm (see Deuteronomy 8:12-14; Jeremiah 6:16; Hosea 6:4; Malachi 3:7; 2 Peter 2:20-21; Revelation 2:4)?

2. What are some ways we can keep ourselves from becoming lukewarm (see Deuteronomy 4:9; Hebrews 3:13; 12:15; 1 John 1:9; Revelation 3:2)?

3. Perhaps you are not lukewarm, but are there areas of your spiritual life you would like to improve upon?

4. What does Galatians 2:20 say? What is of greatest significance to you in this verse?

5. How might you overcome evil with goodness?

6. What steps can you take, in the days ahead, to live out the crucified life more passionately?

6

Deepening the Relationship

"You will call, and the LORD will answer;
you will cry, and He will say, 'Here I am.'"
—ISAIAH 58:9

The story I'm about to share is a hard one to tell. It's about a woman named Ann Saunders, whose deep relationship with Jesus carried her through a most horrendous trial. The details are difficult to write (and some of them I am keeping out). Though this account may be hard to read, I share it because we can learn from Ann's experiences that even in most difficult circumstances, God can work mightily and gloriously and do His good work—though we may not understand why or how He is doing that work.

For years, Captain John Kendall had commanded his cargo ship from Liverpool to St. John, New Brunswick, then back to Liverpool without incident. The journey was rather safe, and Mrs. Kendall decided to accompany her husband on one of the trips. James Friar, one of the seamen who worked for the captain, invited his fiancée, Ann Saunders, to also join them on this trip. She hesitantly agreed to do so. They, along with 19 seamen, left for St. John on November 10, 1825.

The trip to St. John was noneventful, although the first three days Ann experienced seasickness. After that she adjusted to the sea and enjoyed the rest of the voyage to St. John. Once at St. John, Captain Kendall ordered his seamen to load up the ship with a cargo of timber. Ann said of the seamen,

> Many of the seamen were married and had left in Europe numerous families dependent on them for support. Alas! poor mortals, little did they probably think, when they bid their loving companions and their tender little ones the last adieu, that it was to be a final one and that they were to behold their faces no more in this frail world! But we must not charge an infinitely wise and good God foolishly, who cannot err, but orders every event for the best.[1]

On January 18, 1826, the wind was favorable for the cargo ship to set sail back home to Liverpool. Unfortunately, on the first of February, a severe storm arose. It blew away some of the timber, some spars on the vessel, and even washed one of the boats off the deck. Worse yet, some of the seamen were severely wounded. When the storm subsided, Mrs. Kendall and Ann spent the day dressing the wounds of the injured, while those who escaped injury cleared the deck of the broken spars, splicing and disentangling the rigging.

Four days later, another storm came upon the ship, more severe than the last. The massive and violent seas swept almost every movable article from the deck, and threw one of the seamen overboard. Fortunately he was rescued. A few moments later, the whole of the ship's stern was damaged. Ann said, "This was only the beginning of a scene of horrid calamities, doubly horrible to me, who had never before witnessed anything so awful."[2]

While the captain and officers were on deck discussing what could be done to protect their lives, Mrs. Kendall and Ann were on their knees, praying. Ann remarked that both the women enjoyed "a share of God's great mercy."[3]

The following morning the storm redoubled in vigor. Nothing mattered now except to preserve lives. The crew did all they could to save the 60 pounds of bread and the few pounds of cheese that were still in storage. Because the cabin was nearly filled with water, everyone had to remain above deck. That evening the sea was almost breaking over them, and there were unremitting streams of lightning and frightful peals of thunder.

When daylight returned, the bad dream wasn't over. One of the poor seamen, overcome by fatigue, was discovered hanging lifeless by some part of the rigging. As his body was committed to the deep, Ann was thinking that soon it would be her own turn to be buried in the sea.

At 6:00 AM everyone's depressed spirits were revived by the appearance of a boat coming toward them. It proved to be an American vessel that remained in their view that entire day, trying to get near enough to rescue them. Unfortunately, because the seas were so rough, the ship simply could not get near—so it left.

Ann said, "It would be impossible for me to attempt to describe the feelings of all on board at this moment, on seeing so unexpectedly vanish the pleasing hope of being rescued by this vessel from our perilous situation."[4]

After the boat disappeared, some of the men discovered spare canvas and used it to make a tent. While this relieved everyone a bit, their situation was still dismal, for food rations had been limited to a quarter of a biscuit a day.

On February 8, as the rough seas continued, everyone noticed a large ship at a great distance. Captain Kendall ordered a signal of distress to be sent, and soon they noticed the large brig approaching them. Everyone was greatly encouraged—unfortunately, the storm caused the ship to go in the opposite direction. By nightfall, they saw the brig no more.

On February 11, another vessel was spotted, but it didn't come close to them, and was quickly out of sight.

As the days came and went, everyone on board was gradually perishing, due to their provisions having been depleted. Hunger and thirst began to select their victims, and the seamen who died were committed to the deep.

The living knew they needed food to sustain them. So they all agreed (even those who eventually would die) that the bodies of the dead could no longer be buried in the sea. Ann said,

> As the calls of hunger had now become too importunate to be resisted, it is a fact, although shocking to relate, that we were reduced to the awful extremity to attempt to support our feeble bodies a while longer by subsisting on the dead body of the deceased.[5]

Ann had the miserable job of preserving the meat from those bodies. Yet her faith sustained her. She said, "We had nothing to hope from human aid but only from the mercy of the Almighty, whose ways are unsearchable."[6]

More and more people died, some of them going raving mad before doing so. In the midst of all this, Ann credits the Almighty for giving her the ability to spend her moments praying with those who were still alive and helping them prepare for eternity.[7]

The most agonizing pain for Ann had to be watching her fiancé die and then having to use his body to help the others survive. Her misery was unimaginable. She wrote,

> Judge then, my female readers (for it is you that can best judge) what must have been my feelings, to see a youth for whom I had formed an indissoluable attachment—

him with whom I expected so soon to be joined in wed-
lock and to spend the remainder of my days—expiring
before my eyes for the want of that sustenance which
nature requires for the support of life and which it was
not in my power to afford him. And myself at the same
moment so far reduced by hunger and thirst as to be
driven to the horrid alternative to preserve my own life
to plead my claim to the greater portion of his precious
blood as it oozed half congealed from the wound inflicted
upon his lifeless body![8]

Ann added,

"Oh, this was a bitter cup indeed! But it was God's will
that it should not pass me—and God's will must be done.
O, it was a chastening rod that has been the means, I
trust, of weaning me forever from all the vain enjoyments
of this frail world.[9]

On February 26, an English ship came into sight. The usual signals
of distress were sent. Even though the sea was calm and the winds less
boisterous, to everyone's inexpressible grief, the ship did not offer any
assistance. The survivors sat dejectedly on their slowly sinking ship as
the other vessel drifted out of sight.

By now, more than two-thirds of the crew had perished. The
remaining six were weak, distracted, and destitute of almost everything.
Ann said they were actually envying the fate of the lifeless corpses.[10]

Early in the morning of March 7, a sail was spotted on the horizon.
The ship's crew, with Ann's assistance, made all the signals of distress
that their little remaining strength could muster up. Ann said, "But,
praised be God, the hour of our deliverance had now arrived."[11]

The ship that saved Ann and the remaining crew was the HMS *Blonde*, which belonged to Captain George Anson (Lord) Byron (a cousin of the British poet George Gordon Byron, 1788–1824). As the six survivors were being helped onto Lord Byron's ship, the lieutenant of the HMS *Blonde* looked over their sinking vessel. He saw slices of fresh meat spread on the quarterdeck and said, "You have yet, I perceive, fresh meat."[12] He was sickened when he found out it wasn't animal meat that had sustained the survivors. Lord Byron's entire crew pitied these poor people who had been through so much. Ann said the crew treated them with great kindness, "insomuch that we soon gained our strength to that degree as to be able in ten days after to go on board of a vessel bound to Europe."[13]

Ann ends her story by saying, "I think I can truly say I had witnessed and endured more of the heavy judgments and afflictions of this world than any other of its female inhabitants."[14]

The Importance of Trusting God

You may be struggling, wondering, *Why would God allow Ann to go through such a horrendous experience?* I admit I've had that same thought, too. Why does He allow *any* of us to go through difficult times? Why did He ask Abraham to leave his home and move far away to a foreign place? Why did He allow Shadrach, Meshach, and Abendego to be thrown into a fiery furnace? Why did He allow John the Baptist to be beheaded? We will probably never know the answers—at least, not on this side of heaven. But this is where trust in the Lord begins…right?

As we know, trust is everything in a relationship. I can imagine how hurt my husband Brian would feel if I didn't trust him. We all want to be relied on. We do our best to earn trust in others by keeping our promises and showing ourselves honorable in our actions.

If we are so apt to trust those close to us, how much more should we, the bride of Christ, trust our Groom, the One who loves us most? Our Beloved is "our refuge and strength, a very present help in trouble" (Psalm 46:1-2). "No good thing does He withhold" from us (Psalm 84:11). As we trust in Him in our situation, "he shall bring it to pass" (Psalm 37:5 KJV) and promises to "make your paths straight" (Proverbs 3:6). We are told that as we trust, we will be blessed (Psalm 40:4).

Job trusted God despite losing his children and livestock and experiencing terrible physical affliction. In the end, he was helped and blessed (Job 42:10-17). We can take our hardships and withdraw

> *F*aith is believing in Jesus, believing His Word, and believing in His promises.

from God, but then we won't know His blessing. Instead we will be driven to despair because we don't have a Helper. When we trust God, we find a hiding place and a rock of defense. He is our Refuge, He becomes our Strength. And how foolish it would be for us to forget Jesus, especially during our times of need. He is our help when all other help fails.

Trust is what allows the deepening of any relationship. So imagine then how grieved Jesus must feel when people don't believe in Him, or do not "trust in His salvation" (Psalm 78:22). Remember Jesus' comment to the father who had a demon-possessed son? Jesus told him, "All things are possible to him who believes" (Mark 9:23). And sadly, even the disciples fell short when it came to trusting Jesus. Their trust should have been strong because they walked with Him every day, observed Him performing miracles, and saw Him take care of all who came to Him for help. Yet despite all that, their faith was still weak.

And what about *our* trust in Jesus? If it's weak, our spiritual passion will be hindered. How can we strengthen our faith and deepen our trust? There are three steps we can take to accomplish this: remember God's help, call upon the Lord, and endure in faith.

How to Strengthen Our Faith

Remember God's Help

When Jesus tells us to have faith (Mark 11:22), He is telling us to have *complete trust* in Him. That's what faith is. It's believing in Jesus, believing His Word, and believing in His promises. It's believing He has our best in mind. And when our faith or trust in Jesus is weak, we grieve Him. For good reason, that's why it's so important for us to build up our faith and deepen our trust.

Unfortunately, we don't always recognize our lack of faith. That was certainly true of the disciples, as we saw in chapter 2. You'll recall Jesus was asleep and they were, to put it mildly, frantic! Jesus asked them, "How is it that you have no faith?" (Mark 4:40).

On another occasion, the disciples realized their lack of faith. Because they spent day after day with Christ, they could see His incredible spiritual power. In regard to the power to forgive, they begged, "Increase our faith!" (Luke 17:5). A few days later, the Lord answered their plea in a very direct way.

Picture the scene: The disciples and Christ had traveled across the Sea of Galilee. It wasn't until they got to the other side that they realized they had forgotten to bring bread with them (Matthew 16:5). So they discussed their lack of bread among themselves. Desirous to get the conversation more on a spiritual plane, Christ interrupted the disciples' discussion with a caution: "Watch out and beware of the leaven of the Pharisees and Saducees" (verse 6).

Then, as incredible as this sounds, rather than question, probe, and seek heavenly teaching about Christ's metaphor of the leaven, the disciples went back to their discussion about having no bread (verse 7). Perhaps a bit frustrated, Christ said,

> You men of little faith, why do you discuss among your-
> selves that you have no bread? Do you not yet under-

stand or remember the five loaves of the five thousand, and how many baskets full you picked up? Or the seven loaves of the four thousand, and how many large baskets full you picked up? (Matthew 16:8-10).

Imagine how hurt Jesus must have felt realizing that in spirit, the disciples were far from Him. How could they so quickly forget the miraculous feeding of thousands of people—which they had personally witnessed? This time the disciples' request for an ever-increasing faith would be realized. But how? By Christ's probing question: "Do you not yet understand or remember?" (Matthew 16:9). This question served as a catalyst that prompted the disciples to realize that their perspective of *present* circumstances should be based upon remembering God's help in *past* situations.

Thus, the moral of the story for us today is simple but all too easily forgotten. If we desire to deepen our faith, we need to focus not upon current circumstances, but upon God's help in past situations.

Ann Saunders, when her life was in great danger, had a sustaining faith because she remembered God's great mercy and was thankful for it. Because of this, she was able to see God's mercy and grace at work on that ship, even though there were no overtly visible signs of God's help.

When we remember God's past help, we become confident He will use our present difficult circumstances for our good and His glory. John Bunyan (author of *Pilgrim's Progress*), while in the midst of a difficult trial, desperately wanted relief from his troubles. He said that one evening, while he was at a meeting with other believers, he was full of sadness and terror. Suddenly he remembered the Lord's words in 2 Corinthians 12:9—words that came upon him with great power: "My grace is sufficient for thee; my grace is sufficient for thee; my grace is sufficient for thee."[15]

He said, "Oh! Methought that every word was a mighty word unto me; as 'my', and 'grace,' and 'sufficient,' and 'for thee'; they were then, and sometimes are still, far bigger than others be."[16]

Those powerful words helped Bunyan endure his trial and trust Jesus in greater ways. Those same words can help us—and with them we find a promise. Not only did the Lord say, "My grace is sufficient for you," He added that "power is perfected in weakness" (verse 9).

> *It's the tough times in life that help prove whether our faith is for real or not.*

The apostle Paul was glad for his weakness, "so that the *power of Christ* may dwell in me" (verse 9). He came to see that the power of Christ in him was more important than freedom from the insults, distresses, persecutions, and difficulties that came his way (verse 10). As Paul *remembered* Christ's power and dwelled on it, he *saw* that power work mightily in his life. So, too, can it be with us. God's grace is ours, and His power is ours. And like Paul, we can see this grace and power at work when trials come into our lives. This is why the Lord allows us to experience difficulties.

It's the tough times in life that help prove whether our faith is for real or not. They help reveal whether we are following Jesus out of love or out of mere impulse—whether we are acting out of love for Him or for ourselves. Jesus Himself said that trials will come (Luke 14:25-33). Those who can't endure will indeed walk away: "As a result of this many of His disciples withdrew" (John 6:66).

Keep in mind that God does not promise that He will remove our troubles. He is looking for the greatest good for us. While we may consider our troubling circumstances to be of primary importance, God doesn't. This doesn't mean He doesn't care—not at all! He cares tremendously. He wants to carry our burdens (Psalm 55:22). But to Him, our troubles are secondary. *Our spiritual growth is of first importance.*

We can also strengthen our faith when we...

Call upon the Lord

Most of us cannot imagine being able to endure the weight of a horrendous trial. Yet when that trial comes, we *can* endure if we respond to the Lord's plea: "Call upon Me in the day of trouble; I shall rescue you" (Psalm 50:15). And there's more! He also says, "You will call, and the LORD will answer; you will cry, and He will say, 'Here I am'" (Isaiah 58:9). What comfort! The Lord is with you, He will rescue you, He will answer you. In your tears, He will comfort you. Such help as this is that of a groom toward his bride. All he desires to do is to protect and strengthen her soul. Jesus, our Groom, does strengthen us as we call upon Him. He makes known to us the greatness of His power; He revives our soul and renews our hope, our confidence, our courage. He gives us His all-sufficient grace for whatever we must go through.

We certainly saw this in the life of Ann Saunders. Imagine if she had lacked trust while on that ship, never calling upon God, believing that He had abandoned her. She would have been drowning in doubt and would have never thought about reaching out to others with God's grace. As well, her life after her rescue would have, most likely, been filled with bitterness toward God rather than praise. Ann was able to praise God because she knew of His goodness: "I will give You thanks with all my heart; I will sing praises to You.... And give thanks to Your name for Your lovingkindness and Your truth; for You have magnified Your word according to all Your name" (Psalm 138:1-2).

Each one of us, whether we are up or down, should have a perpetuity of praise all the days of our life. Wouldn't it be strange to experience a day in which there was *nothing* to praise God for? A day of no new mercy, no new grace, no new favor, no fresh deliverance from our sins and trouble. What a horrible day that would be! Fortunately, no such day exists. "Every day I will bless You, and I will praise Your name forever and ever" (Psalm 145:2). My friend Debbie Fisher, during her dying hour, still saw God's great mercy and continually praised Jesus. Just moments before she died, she was singing praises to Him. She died with the name of Jesus on her breath.

Both Ann Saunders and Debbie Fisher had a deep sense of all that God was to them, and all that they were to Him. They knew that God was "intimately acquainted with all my ways" (Psalm 139:3). They knew He was never far from them: "You will call, and the LORD will answer; you will cry, and the He will say, 'Here I am'" (Isaiah 58:9). They knew He was interested in what they were going through. They knew He cared for them *at all times*. They said, with the psalmist, "The LORD is my rock and my fortress and my deliverer, my God, my rock, in whom I take refuge" (Psalm 18:2). When Ann was on that sinking ship, when Debbie lay dying on her bed, they couldn't help but have a fervent zeal that publicly expressed their passion for God and His unending grace. Both women passed the testing of their faith (James 1:1-5) with the help of a very important commodity: endurance.

Endure in Faith

When we turn to the Lord in a trial, rather than panic, He will enable us to endure. *Endurance* is the power to withstand hardship or stress; it's the ability to continue trusting the Lord all through an ordeal. Endurance enables us to be patient and to tolerate trouble or suffering without becoming angry or upset.

As trials come and go, our ability to endure will grow stronger and stronger. The Lord blesses us with this endurance so that we will lack nothing spiritually. He says, "Let endurance have its perfect result, so that you may be perfect and complete, lacking in nothing" (James 1:4). Through the trials we encounter, the Lord works to supply our present lack. If we lack in a certain character trait—such as patience, love, or gentleness—God can use life's challenges to help build us up.

I'm convinced Ann Saunders was well prepared for the trial she faced because of previous trials that had helped build her endurance—such as experiencing the death of her father as a young girl, and seeing her mother give away three of her siblings because she lacked the resources to care for them. In the midst of her difficult experiences, Ann was never bitter. Rather, she was thankful to the Lord for the blessings she had received from Him.

Certainly the Lord wouldn't have allowed Ann on that horrific journey if He thought she wasn't ready for it. He only gives us what we can bear. Ann's enduring faith was ready to praise the Almighty while in the pit of despair, ready to passionately live out her faith before the seamen who were dying around her, and ready to help prepare many of those men for eternity. I'm sure that the men who accepted Jesus as a result of her witness were thankful to the Lord for having put Ann on that cargo ship.

How might your current testing benefit others? How are you benefiting? Is the testing of your faith drawing you closer to Jesus? Is it deepening your relationship with Him? It is so much better for our faith to be tested so that our ability to endure can be strengthened. When we run from trials and doubt God, we are running away from Jesus and His help. And we miss out on receiving spiritual blessings.

The Strategy of Going Step-by-Step

Our trials are like a ladder. From here to heaven, it's a long way up. We cannot reach the top merely by looking upward. Rather, we must climb the ladder. It's only by taking one step at a time that we make progress. And because it's overwhelming to think about the many steps ahead, we need to focus on taking just one step at a time.

Consider King David. When he was in the dumps, he took one step at a time by thinking about what God had done for him, what He is like, and even what God had done for the nation of Israel. He meditated upon God's faithfulness to him, and as a result, David's faith increased as he recognized that God would indeed take care of him.

Ann Saunders, too, took her trials one step at a time. She started by praying, and then she dwelled upon God's great mercy. Her trust in the Lord became so strong that she had not only the divine power to endure the horrible ordeal, but also the insight to see what God was doing in her life. She said He was "weaning me forever from all the vain enjoyments of this frail world."[17]

Here are some simple steps we can take when we're faced with adversity:

Step 1: *Accept* what God says in His Word and never doubt Him (Hebrews 6:18).

Step 2: *Remember* God's past mercies and praise Him for them (Psalm 143:5; Romans 4:21).

Step 3: *Believe* in God's promises rather than be overwhelmed by what seems impossible (Romans 4:21; 8:28).

Step 4: *Trust* God's way for your life, and know that He is leading you in the direction He wants you to go, and that *everything* will work together for your good (Psalm 37:5; Proverbs 3:5-6; Romans 8:28).

When we take these steps, our faith can grow passionate and strong, and our relationship with Jesus will become marked by a deeper trust—like that of a bride toward her groom, whom she never doubts or questions.

He Maketh No Mistake

My Father's way may twist and turn,
My heart may throb and ache.
But in my soul I'm glad I know,
He maketh no mistake.

My cherished plans may go astray,
My hopes may fade away,
But still I'll trust my Lord to lead
For He doth know the way.

Tho' night be dark and it may seem
That day will never break;
I'll pin my faith, my all in Him.
He maketh no mistake.

There's so much now I cannot see,
My eyesight's far too dim;
But come what may, I'll simply trust
And leave it all to Him.

For by and by the mist will lift
And plain it all He'll make,
Through all the way, tho' dark to me,
He made not one mistake.[18]

Our Passion in Action

1. In what areas of your life is your faith weak? In what ways do you find it most dificult to trust in Jesus?

2. What spiritual blessing would you like to ask God for? Are you willing to accept a trial that will help you gain the spiritual blessing you desire? Why or why not?

3. Are you currently going through a trial? Take the step-by-step approach: What does God say from His Word that can help you during this time? What can you remember of God's past mercies? Can you, this day, praise Him for those mercies? What promise of God can you claim during this trial? How might He be working everything together for your good?

4. How might your past or present trial help someone else? How has it helped you?

Giving Him All Your Love

"*I love You, O LORD, my strength.*"
—PSALM 18:1

Hermann Samuel Reimarus (1694–1768) was a professor of theology in Hamburg, Germany. He had a sterling reputation and was cherished and loved by all. Christians admired him, the clergy respected him, and church members enjoyed fellowshipping with him.

When Reimarus died, the eulogy given at his funeral may well have spoken of his great passionate love for the Almighty. And as the people watched the casket go into the ground, those who were believers most likely had a calm assurance that his body couldn't be locked up in the grave because of profession of faith and belief in the resurrection.

Six years later, there was a great shock—heartbreaking for Christians—at the revelation of a 4,000-page manuscript on which Reimarus had worked for 20 years. In it he claimed Christianity was nothing but a fraud invented by Christ's disciples,[1] and that all the biblical miracles were fraudulent and the supposed revelations were sheer invention.[2] He also believed that Jesus was a fanatic and that when He cried on the cross, "My God, My God, why have You forsaken me?" this was Christ's "confession of his error and bitter defeat."[3] He also wrote,

The failure of that Messianic mission and Jesus' inglorious death on the Cross shattered the disciples' expectations. Faced with a crisis, the apostles concocted the account of Jesus as the expected Jewish suffering savior who came to redeem humanity from sin and would be raised on the third day. The resurrection story was thus a fraud, perpetrated by the disciples after they had stolen Jesus' body from the tomb. And so it happened that Jesus' mission and message—that of a discredited apocalyptic fanatic—was reshaped by the disciples' invention of an entirely new religion, wholly foreign to Jesus' own intention.[4]

It was Reimarus's daughter who found the manuscript and allowed her father's friend, philosopher G.E. Lessing, to publish the manuscript *on the condition* that its author remain anonymous. Lessing not only agreed to keep the author anonymous, but said he would claim that he had found the manuscript in a library where he was working at the time. Despite the agreement, the truth of the manuscript's authorship soon got out.

Shortly thereafter, everyone knew the real Reimarus—not the pious man who seemed to enjoy the company of clergymen, not the seemingly godly scholar, but the hater of Christianity, a mocker of its Scripture, an enemy "of the cross of Christ" (Philippians 3:18).

If ever there was a hypocritical life, it was Reimaruss'. The public would never have known the real man had the manuscript gone unpublished or had his name not been attached to it. What a lesson for those who revered the theology professor! They discovered that a person could claim to be serving the kingdom of God, but not really be serving God at all.

We, too, can learn from this lesson. A person's "spiritual" character, though seen in the eyes of others as superb, may not be pleasing to God. Many of us could easily conclude that a woman who is volunteering at church, serving in the choir, or participating in women's Bible classes is demonstrating her love for Jesus, but we must realize that a person's actions are not always a reliable test of one's love for God. Any one of us could be involved in ministry for show, or to advance our personal agenda, or for some other wrong motive. Christ looks not at our ministry, but our heart.

Another lesson we can learn from looking at Reimarus is that a very important part of loving God is loving Him in truth. God is truth (Isaiah 65:16); therefore, we are to walk in truth (3 John 4) and worship in truth (John 4:23). Truth is imperative. If our knowledge of the Lord isn't based upon biblical truth, then we don't have true faith, nor salvation, nor God (2 John 9). We must make sure our beliefs are based upon truth from the Bible. For instance, if I were to say, "I'm going to heaven because I am a good person," then I am not loving God in truth. Why? Because *God's way* is grace, not good works. He tells us we can't get to heaven by being a good person (Ephesians 2:8-9).

If I say to you, "All paths lead to heaven; we will all get there one way or another," then again I am not loving God in truth. Jesus said, "I am the way, and the truth, and the life; no one comes to the Father but through Me" (John 14:6). Jesus made it clear there is no other way to heaven except through Him. You *must* believe in Him to have everlasting life (1 John 5:11-12).

Nor would I be loving God in truth if I said I believe in extrabiblical teaching—that is, extra "scriptures" along with the Bible. All extra "scriptures" are contrary to the Word of God, and if we were to trust in them, we would not be loving God, nor would we truly have Him. As the Bible tells us, "Anyone who goes too far and does not abide in the teaching of Christ, does not have God" (2 John 9). We have a very clear warning from God's Word, the Bible: "I testify to everyone who hears the words of the prophecy of this book: if anyone adds to them, God will add to him the plagues which are written in this book"

(Revelation 22:18-19). God's Word alone is the source of truth (Psalm 119:160; John 17:17). God wants us to abide only in His Word, and His truth has been given to us once and for all (Jude 3). No other outside "truth" is to be added to what we are given in the Bible.

Because Reimarus didn't walk in truth, it goes without saying that he never allowed God to claim his heart. How he fooled others into believing he was a Christian! And this still happens today. People can talk piously about walking the straight and narrow, while in their heart they are as worldly as the person who makes no pretension of living a godly lifestyle. One thing for sure: Reimarus *never* fooled God. Scripture says, "Be sure your sin will find you out" (Numbers 32:23). For good reason we are encouraged to "test yourselves to see if you are in the faith; examine yourselves! Or do you not recognize this about yourselves, that Jesus Christ is in you—*unless indeed you fail the test?*" (2 Corinthians 13:5). If you aren't sure you would pass the test, you'll want to turn to "Do You Belong to Jesus?" on page 227.

For those of us who are abiding in truth, we do have a love for Jesus. Perhaps, though, you are like me, and you desire for your love for Jesus to be more intimate and personal. I have found that whenever I'm desirous to get closer to Jesus, usually there are some obstacles I've allowed to get in the way—obstacles I need to remove. For example, back in chapter 4 we learned about obstacles that keep us from accepting God's love for us. In this chapter, we're going to look at a key obstacle that keeps us from loving Jesus—sin.

Allowing Sin's Presence

When we allow sin in our heart, we are welcoming an intruder into the very place where Christ dwells. We are bringing darkness into the presence of Christ's light. And we quench the Holy Spirit (1 Thessalonians 5:19), who grieves when we sin.

Have you noticed that sin keeps us from loving Jesus? And the consequences of harboring sin within us are miserable! We lose spiritual power to receive godly insight from the Word of God, our morals weaken, and our conscience isn't as sharp. And worst of all, our spiritual passion—our inner drive to zealously live for Jesus—dwindles.

Yet another problem is that sometimes we put on a façade that misrepresents the state of our spiritual life as we conceal sin in our heart. Paul warned, "Let love be without hypocrisy" (Romans 12:9).

To get a better idea of the seriousness of sin, let's look at some people who supposedly were passionate for God, but just one "little" sin got them into a lot of trouble.

Adam, for eating a piece of forbidden fruit, was condemned to exhausting labor, his wife would suffer in childbirth, and both were thrown out of paradise (Genesis 3:11-19).

Lot's wife, for looking back, was turned into a pillar of salt (Genesis 19:26). As a warning, we're told to "remember Lot's wife" (Luke 17:32).

Moses, for taking credit for something God did, was forbidden to enter the Promised Land (Numbers 20:7-12).

Uzzah, for touching the ark (because the oxen nearly upset it), was struck dead (1 Chronicles 13:9-10).

Zacharias, for unbelief, was struck speechless for nine months (Luke 1:18-20).

Ananias and Sapphira, for one lie, were struck dead (Acts 5:3-5,7-10).

There is more to these "little" sins than meets the eyes. Ultimately, sin is an issue of the heart. Whatever we love most, that we do. If we love pleasure most, our character is sensual; if we love possessions most, our character is worldly; if we love God most, our character is godly. As the old saying goes, "Acts make habits; habits make character."

The presence of sin in us can make us two-faced Christians, allowing people to think we are one way while, in reality, we are another. For example, Ananias and Sapphira wanted the church to think they were big givers when, in fact, they held back some of their money. They wanted to give others one impression, while at heart, that impression wasn't really true about them.

What are other examples of this kind of behavior? There are some Christian couples who date and go to church together, but secretly they are involved in premarital sex. Although they know how wrong their sin is, they rationalize it. They obviously do not love Jesus, for He said, "He who does not love Me does not keep My words" (John 14:24).

Another common problem is women in the church who slander and gossip. In every form of gossip, the whole story is not being told to the third party. Part of the truth is being suppressed or misrepresented. Because love to God is influenced by truth, *nothing* should ever lead us to communicate a false, or partial, or misleading representation of the facts. And Scripture plainly tells us, "Let all...slander be put away from you" (Ephesians 4:31), and "Let no unwholesome word proceed from your mouth" (verse 29).

If we are holding on to a sin in us, whatever it may be, we need to take heed: "If I regard wickedness in my heart, the Lord will not hear" (Psalm 66:18). As mentioned a few chapters ago, sin disqualifies us from God listening to us. And not only will God not hear, but we ourselves will have a difficult time praying. Sin deadens our spiritual life, keeping us "silent" about our sin (Psalm 32:3).

When we focus on indulging in sin rather than on loving Jesus, we have no power to throw aside our sin—power that makes the enticement of sin to be weak, and the overwhelming drive to love Jesus be strong. So let's take heed of the warning, "Sin is crouching at the door; and its desire is for you, but you must master it" (Genesis 4:7). And master it we will as we keep our heart pure, remain true to our high calling as Christians and, more importantly, our title "bride of Christ." Don't let sin be an obstacle between you and Jesus.

Once the obstacle of sin is removed, we're ready to work on strengthening our love for Jesus.

Understanding Love for God

Mark was deeply troubled about his spiritual well-being because he didn't seem to have an intense love for God. He confessed this to his Christian friend and co-worker Joe:

> When I go home from here, I expect to take my baby on my knee, look into her sweet eyes, listen to her charming prattle, and, tired as I am, her presence will rest me; for I love that child with unutterable tenderness. But she loves me little. If my heart were breaking, it would not disturb her sleep. If my body were racked with pain, it would not interrupt her play. If I were dead, she would forget me in a few days. Besides this, she has never brought me a penny, but has been a constant expense to me. I am not rich, but there is not enough money in the world to buy my baby. How is it? Does she love me, or do I love her? Do I withhold my love until I know she loves me? Am I waiting for her to do something worthy of my love before extending it?[5]

> *When we dwell on how much God loves us, it compels us to love Him in return.*

This illustration of the love of our heavenly Father for His children caused tears to roll down Mark's face. He came to understand that it is *not* his love of God he should be thinking about, *but God's love for him.* Isn't this the real issue for us all? It's not how intensely we love God, but how intensely He loves us. When we dwell on how much God loves us, it compels us to love Him in return.

This is confirmed in 1 John 4:10,19, which says, "This is love, not that we loved God, but that He loved us....We love because He first loved us."

The fact that we love in response to God's love became especially evident to me when I met Luwan. Years ago as I was passing a Thai Buddhist temple, I decided to pull to the side of the road and see if I could go and share Christ with someone on the property. There was no gathering in the temple, but the temple doors were open. Close to the doors was Luwan, a woman in her early twenties. She was all smiles as I approached her and began to chitchat with her. I could tell immediately that she was quite lonely and hungrily welcomed my company.

Luwan had been raised to believe, according to Buddhism, that people either make good or bad karma in their life. Buddhists are also taught that life is a samsara—a perpetual wandering. The transition in this wandering from one life to another is termed *rebirth* (or reincarnation). If you were to talk about being "born again" with a Buddhist, they would think you are referring to reincarnation. They would think you were telling them they would be coming back to earth to relive their suffering all over again, which they view as bad karma. Luwan's only hope was to go into nonexistence in order to avoid suffering. This was her view of "salvation."

Imagine, then, the look on Luwan's face when she heard the message of God's love. We sat down on the steps and I began sharing with her all about the love of God and how Jesus loved us so much that He died for our sins—thus making it possible for us to enjoy an eternal life of bliss with Him in heaven, with no more suffering.

Luwan didn't know much about Jesus, so for more than two hours we talked about Him, His offering of forgiveness of sins, and His invitation for us to come and follow Him. I made it clear that Jesus said He is the only way (John 14:6). Luwan asked, "How can I have this Jesus? How can I live with Him forever?"

Right there on the temple steps, I led Luwan in prayer, and she asked Jesus to forgive her of her sins, and asked Him to always be with her as she followed Him as her Lord and Master.

After Luwan finished, tears were flowing down her face. She gave me a hug, and I gave her my pocket Bible and suggested she start reading the book of John. She hugged that Bible as if it were the greatest treasure (which it is!). I also told her about a strong Bible-believing church she could attend, which for her, was within walking distance of the temple. How excited she was!

Luwan had been taught to follow a man who offered her no peace, no hope, no truth, and no love. In return, Luwan

> *Intimacy is based upon how well you and the one you love know each another.*

never had any love for Buddha. But after hearing about Jesus and His great love for her, Luwan *loved* Jesus. She desperately wanted to follow Him.[6]

Again, it's when we focus on the Lord's great love for us that we are compelled to show greater love in return. Consider these words from Isaiah 53:5: "He was pierced through for our transgressions, He was crushed for our iniquities; the chastening for our well-being fell upon Him, and by His scourging we are healed." Doesn't the truth of Christ's great sacrifice for you prompt instant love?

How is your love for the Lord right now? Do you see room for growth? Perhaps you'll find it helpful to evaluate your love by taking an "intimacy test."

Growing in Intimacy

When Brian and I were engaged, a pastor serving as our premarital counselor gave us a compatibility test. For what it's worth, we scored high, showing that we knew one another quite well—*very* well. We were told, by the results of the test, that we pretty much see eye to eye on everything. The pastor, as he went over the test results with us, said, "It's obvious your love for one another is strong."

This brings us to a key point: Intimacy is based upon how well you and the one you love know each another. The better you know one another, the greater your potential to have a stronger love. If you read chapter 4, you already know that Jesus' love for you is strong. Consider how well He knows you: the exact number of hairs on your head (Matthew 10:30), all that you do (Psalm 139:1-3), your every thought (Psalm 139:2), everything about you (Psalm 139:4). And the greatest evidence of His love for you is the fact He died for you.

Now, how strong is your love for Jesus? Let's take the intimacy test: Do I obey Jesus wholeheartedly (John 14:21)? Do I trust His divine power completely (Hebrews 1:3)? Do I meditate on His glory (Psalm 57:7-11)? Do I seek His fellowship (1 Corinthians 1:9)? Am I sensitive to how He feels (Psalm 69:9)? Do I love what He loves (Jeremiah 10:24)? Do I love whom He loves (1 John 5:1)? Do I hate what He hates (Psalm 97:10)?[7]

No matter how we do on this test, there's always room to enhance our love for our Lord. And there are a number of ways we can grow in our love.

Intimacy Through Devotion

Remember, the more we know someone, the more we come to love him or her. And to know Jesus means we come to understand what moves Him, what He's passionate about, what's important to Him. This means making Jesus the chief affection of our heart, above all others. Jesus wants it that way: "He who loves father or mother more than Me is not worthy of Me; and he who loves son or daughter more than Me is not worthy of Me" (Matthew 10:37). He also said, "Everyone who has left houses or brothers or sisters or father or mother or children or farms for My name's sake, will receive many times as much, and will inherit eternal life" (Matthew 19:29).

Clearly, Jesus seeks the devotion of our heart.

Intimacy Through Confession

Confession is so wonderful! It keeps our relationship with Jesus free from all barriers. Ideally, we want to go to the Lord in confession daily. Any attitude, any unwholesome word, any wrong tone of voice, any possible offense ought to be acknowledged so that nothing hinders our relationship with Him.

While sin deadens the spiritual life, confession rejuvenates it and brings us into a more intimate relationship with Jesus. King David prayed, "Create in me a clean heart, O God, and renew a steadfast spirit within me" (Psalm 51:10). He said this after his adulterous affair with Bathsheba and murder of her husband. Would we be able to fully comprehend the magnitude of this request had we not known the dark record of David's heinous sins? I don't think so. Here we have an adulterer and murderer asking for complete cleansing and, along with that, a new spirit.

I also love the fact David used the word "create." In his request for cleansing, he wants everything brand new. He doesn't want to merely dust off his old heart, the old spirit, the old person. No, he wants everything new. So, too, can we have our heart, our spirit, our attitudes—just like on the day we became Christians. Like David, we too can have "the joy of [His] salvation" (Psalm 51:10).

Intimacy Through Praise

Our love for Jesus shows itself best in our gratitude and praise for Him—for what He *has* done for us, *is* doing for us, and *will* do for us. Remember, He is the One who moves mountains and calms the seas, and has us in the palm of His hand! What praise can we offer Him? The psalmist exhorts us, "Sing praise to the LORD, you His godly ones, and give thanks to His holy name" (Psalm 30:4). All through the Psalms we find many men filled with praise for God. King David vowed he was going to praise God "yet more and more" (Psalm 71:14). Habakkuk gives us many reasons to praise God. We can praise His person (Habakkuk 3:1-3), His power (Habakkuk 3:4-7), His purpose (Habakkuk 3:8-16), and praise because of faith in God (Habakkuk 3:17-19). Samuel exhorts us to "consider what great things He has done for you" (1 Samuel 12:24). What great things can you praise Him for?

Praise allows us to grow more in love with Jesus because we are focusing upon what He has done in our lives.

Intimacy Through Love in Action

The apostle Peter, on three separate occasions, denied that he was a disciple of Christ (John 18:17,25,27). During that dark time, Peter's actions did not in any way demonstrate love for the One who was, at that very moment, being rejected, spat on, and crucified for him. Of course, Jesus, who knows our hearts, knew that Peter really loved Him. But such love has to have to be demonstrated through our actions. When the resurrected Jesus talked to Peter about his denials and his love, He didn't say, "Peter, just love Me whatever way you want." No, He was very specific. He told Peter, "Tend My lambs.... Shepherd My sheep.... Tend My sheep" (John 21:15-18). Jesus called Peter to action.

So a strong love for Jesus means more than having inward feelings about Him or saying we love Him. We're to show our love in action. That's what Jesus did. He backed up His words with action. When He said, "I love you," He acted upon that love by dying on a torturous cross. When He said, "I go to prepare a place for you," He acted upon that promise by going back to heaven, the hard way, via the cross.

So when Jesus says, "If anyone loves Me, he will keep My word" (John 14:23), He is telling us to actively love Him by obeying His Word.

Intimacy by Following the Godly Examples of Others

In the Bible, the Lord commended Jehoshaphat because he followed the example of his father, David (2 Chronicles 17:3). Paul the apostle said, "Brethren, join in *following* my example, and *observe* those who walk according to the pattern you have in us" (Philippians 3:17). He also said, "Be *imitators* of me, just as I also am of Christ" (1 Corinthians 11:1).

While Paul asks us to "follow," "observe," and "imitate" him and others, the apostle James adds to that by giving us examples of those we can look at, such as "the prophets who spoke in the name of the Lord," "the endurance of Job," and the prayer-warrior Elijah (James 5:10-11,17). The idea here is that as we follow the example of more mature believers, we will be motivated or inspired by their love for God.

So another part of pursuing greater intimacy with the Lord is by observing those who are already intimate with Him. And you don't have to limit yourself to Bible characters or living people; you can also be encouraged by reading Christian biographies. History is filled with men and women who were spiritually rich and full of spiritual passion. You may find inspiration as you learn from their perseverance, holiness, humility, prayer, and praise. And as you follow the examples of others—whether living or dead—you will learn new ways to love Jesus.

Exhibiting True Intimacy

The spiritually passionate woman has an inner drive in her to pray more, fast when necessary, confess often, and praise Jesus in everything. She covets the Christian virtues such as compassion, patience, faithfulness, and sacrifice, and actively applies them in her life. Without looking for recognition, she longs to use the character traits that God gives her to make a difference in the lives of others, and to show her love to Him. She has a greater interest than most in those who are ignored by society, such as the poor, the hurting, the socially awkward, knowing that Jesus loves them, too.

She thinks about the examples of those who have gone before her and is desirous to learn from them. It's not surprising then that she could easily become like those she admires most. Her admiration for believers like Corrie ten Boom, who under the reign of Hitler hid Jews at the risk of her own life, results in her willingness to stand up for what is right.

Emulating Augustine may lead her to wisdom; following Mary Magdelene's example, or that of the woman at the well, may cause her to be a zealous evangelist; patterning herself after the apostle John may make her a more loving and gentle person; and modeling herself after the apostle Paul may result in her becoming a more serious and diligent woman.

Most of all, she desires to emulate Jesus because of His perfect example. Her love draws her to think deeply about His life and the words He spoke. He is her example and is close to her heart. To her, it's a small thing if she is regarded highly or remembered fondly by others (1 Corinthians 4:3). Rather, her only concern is what God thinks of her.

Your Heart, Completely His

Reimarus gave his heart to empty philosophy, da Vinci gave his heart to painting, Steinbeck gave his heart to writing, and many others have given their hearts to other passing pursuits. *But you have given your heart to Jesus.* Your growing love, unlike the Louvre in Paris, or the Kensington Palace in London, will never crumble or fade, nor will it ever be forgotten because it is highly prized by God. And, because your heart is completely His, having given Him *all* your love, He strongly supports you (2 Chronicles 16:9) and calls you "My own" (John 10:14). Be encouraged, for

> *as the bridegroom rejoices over the bride,*
> *So your God will rejoice over you* (Isaiah 62:5).

Our Passion in Action

1. Psalm 116 begins with the psalmist saying, "I love the LORD, because...." List all the reasons given in verses 1-16, as to why he loves the Lord. After you're done, do yourself next. Write out, "I love the Lord because...."

2. Is there any hindrance(s) in your life that's keeping you from loving Jesus? For instance, do you find it hard to be open with God? Is it hard to trust that God's plan for your life is the best for you? What can you do right now to eliminate any hindrance(s) you may have?

3. Select one or more of the following verses, and think about what the verse(s) means for you in relation to your love life with Jesus: John 6:56; 14:23; Romans 8:9; 2 Corinthians 13:5; Galatians 2:20; Ephesians 2:22; 5:18; Colossians 1:27; Revelation 3:20.

4. First Samuel 12:24 says, "Consider what great things He has done for you." What great things can you currently praise Jesus for?

5. What godly examples can we find from the following verses: Numbers 12:3; 1 Samuel 3:18; Acts 5:41? Is there a Bible character, or a Christian either in heaven or on earth, whose love for Jesus you truly admire? What is it you admire most about their love? How can you begin following their example? We, too, are encouraged to be examples (Matthew 5:16). How might you be an example for others?

6. Thinking about your spiritual giftedness or how God has blessed you materially, how might you demonstrate your love for Jesus in action? (Try to come up with an idea or two for this week.)

8

$\mathcal{E}$xperiencing $\mathcal{U}$ninterrupted $\mathcal{J}$oy

*"These things I have spoken to you so that My joy may be in you,
and that your joy may be made full."*
—JOHN 15:11

Carolyn had experienced her ups and downs in life. Who hasn't? Yet at the moment, things were going pretty well for her. She was a single mother of a college-age daughter and two teenage sons, and quite content. She did have one concern: She had recently had surgery to remove some suspicious calcium deposits in her left breast. In the operating room, the surgeon did a preliminary pathology on the samples he took. All indications were that Carolyn was cancer free. She was, of course, relieved beyond words. She kept this surgery and her concerns of cancer from her children until the night after the operation. When she shared the news with them, they all rejoiced. But little did this rejoicing family know that the very next day, November 25, 1998 (the day before Thanksgiving), they would enter a living hell.

Carolyn's son, Chris, a senior in high school, had just entered his 8:00 AM science class. His teacher told all the students to go out on the football field to observe an experiment in which a tennis ball would be shot out of a small cannon. During the experiment something went terribly wrong, and the cannon that Chris had been asked to hold exploded. He was on fire.

As Chris struggled for his life, the intense heat was viciously melting off his skin, hair, nose, lips, neck, chest, arms, and hands. His entire upper body was aflame. Fortunately, he instinctively shut his eyes while trying to put out the fire. During what seemed like an eternity as he waited for help, Chris's best friend took notice of him. He quickly took off his sweatshirt and used it to put out the flames.

To make matters worse, because of the severity of Chris's burns, the medical personnel who arrived at the scene made the decision to airlift Chris directly to a burn center when, in fact, he needed to go to a hospital to have a breathing tube put down his throat. Chris's airway was swelling, and the extra time it took to get to the burn center put him in even greater danger as he struggled to breathe. He needed help, and fast! He wondered if he would soon die.

The school called Carolyn, and after she was given the wrong information as to the whereabouts of her son, she was finally at Chris's side in the intensive care unit at the burn center.

Amazingly, at this early time, news of Chris's accident was spreading like fire itself—in the newspapers and on television. Carolyn told me, "You never think you're going to see your son's face on the news."

When Carolyn approached Chris's bed for the first time, she was in shock. Just that morning she remembered seeing her young, handsome son look so energetic. Now he appeared lifeless and was fully bandaged, except for his eyes and mouth. Doctors told Carolyn that Chris's larynx was so severely burned that he probably would never speak again—if he survived. Chris was hooked up to several machines that assisted him with his breathing and monitored his heart.

Carolyn had not spent more than a few hours with Chris before she was called out of his room to be given more devastating news. Two close friends said, "Carolyn, your tests came back positive. You have cancer." That news registered alarm for a moment, but Carolyn dismissed it quickly, saying, "I'll deal with it when Chris gets out of the hospital."

Right about now, after seeing that this chapter is about joy, you might be thinking, *What does this story have to do with joy?* You'll soon see. But before I continue on with Carolyn and Chris's story, let's first take a look at what joy—*divine* joy—is.

Defining Divine Joy

Frequently we hear the phrase, "Jesus, man of sorrows." And that's how many artists have painted Him. In their pictures, there is often no light of triumph in His eyes. This is what the joyless soul looks like. Such a person has no gladness in God, *no life* in Him. He or she has no godward passion. Instead, mere happiness is their aim, and it's not the kind of happiness a Christian aims for. For instance, there is a Chinese proverb that states: "If you want to be happy for a year, get married. If you want to be happy for a lifetime, become a gardener." While most people realize that's rather simplistic thinking, still, their pursuit of happiness is shallow, with no consideration for *true* happiness, which is spiritual and heavenly in nature.

If you're a Christian, you'll know this true happiness started when you first came to Christ. You knew an intense joy that came out of the freshness of becoming "born again" (John 3:3). The Spirit of God, or should we say the Spirit of *Life,* woke you up—the spiritually dead. Having been corrupt in your sins, cynical in your thinking, and selfish in your ways, you were awakened to repentance. And you knew the great joy that comes from knowing you were forgiven!

After repentance, the Spirit filled you with "joy and peace in believing" and caused you to "abound in hope" (Romans 15:13). The brightness of life as a new believer may have led you to think that nothing—*absolutely nothing*—could thwart your joy!

Why could nothing thwart our joy? Because, we, at this time, were pretty much ignorant of the spiritual conflicts that the mature Christian will indeed experience. All we knew was that we were joyful that

Jesus died for us, and thus our emotions for Jesus were sky-high. Our hallelujahs were loud. We sensed an absolute thrill as we shouted the glorious name, *Jesus!*

But eventually we come to realize that such emotional joy comes and goes. Scripture reminds us of this fact: "There is a time to weep, and a time to laugh; a time to mourn, and a time to dance" (Ecclesiastes 3:4). "Is anyone among you suffering? Let him pray. Is anyone cheerful? Let him sing praises" (James 5:13). While emotional joy is fine, Paul the apostle reveals to us a different kind of joy that is more substantial and enduring—he speaks of being "sorrowful yet always rejoicing" (2 Corinthians 6:10). This is an inner joy that enables us to rejoice even in the midst of sorrow, a joy that can sustain us even through the most difficult of circumstances. It's *the joy of Jesus.*

Examining Jesus' Joy

Jesus, just days before His horrible death, talked about joy! How so unlike us when we're faced with hardship! So concerned was Jesus about His disciples' grief on account of His death that He offered them His joy—a joy He offers to us today as well: "These things I have spoken to you so that My joy may be in you" (John 15:11). This joy is not some sort of feeling where we are happy all the time. That's not true joy. The joy Jesus offers is a *spiritual joy* that's connected with the soul. It's a joy that's capable of increasing, a joy that's never liable to exhaustion, a joy that's immortal. It's a joy that can carry us through all circumstances in life, enabling us to face anything. Divine joy is what enabled Jesus to die on the cross: *"Who for the joy set before Him* endured the cross, despising the shame" (Hebrews 12:2).

What was the joy "set before Him"? It was a...

Present joy that glorifies the Father, wanting His will in life, regardless of how difficult His circumstances may be (Matthew 6:9-10).

Sacrificial joy that is concerned about the salvation of others and will do whatever it takes to assist another individual into the kingdom of God. Jesus, who died for the salvation and benefit of others, said, "It is more blessed to give than to receive" (Acts 20:35). What might we give others? Jesus gave us eternal life. So the most blessed gift we can give another is the gospel of Jesus, and encouraging him or her to hope in God.

Future joy that looks forward to heaven. Jesus looked forward to going back to the Father (John 17:11); He looked forward to us being with Him in heaven as well (John 17:24). He could endure the agony of the cross because of the good that lay ahead.

So here we have it: Divine joy comes from glorifying God, being concerned with the salvation of others, and looking toward heaven. This is far from worldly joy, which is empty and short-lived. Divine joy is what helped Jesus endure the cross, and that same joy will help us endure the horrendous trials, the cruel words, and whatever else makes up the cross we are to carry (Matthew 16:24).

> *It's* not easy to live above our circumstances, but it can be done.

Perhaps right now, you are enduring some difficult circumstances. You might find it hard to believe that you can really have divine joy in your life. You might be right—you might not be able to experience this joy right now not because it doesn't exist, but because there's an obstacle in your life that hinders you from receiving it.

Unfortunately, many of us are hindered from receiving Christ's joy in full, from understanding more deeply the reality of this joy, and from grasping to a greater degree how we have access to it. And what is it that hinders us? It's principally one main obstacle: We are living beneath our circumstances and being controlled by them, rather than living above our circumstances and exerting control over them. When we are controlled by our circumstances, we cannot live as women of spiritual passion because we're more concerned with our situation and the things connected to it rather than spiritual pursuits.

It's not easy to live above our circumstances, but it can be done. How? We must 1) give our burdens to Jesus; 2) confront our pain; 3) accept our situation; 4) change our thinking; 5) focus on God.

Living Above Our Circumstances

Giving Jesus Our Burdens

Years ago, a missionary to China, whom we'll call Elsa, wrote the following motto:

> Whatever my Father sends me, be it joy or disappointment, no matter how hard it may be to bear, since I know it comes from my Father, I am going to receive it with both hands joyfully.[1]

As time went on, Elsa began to get disappointed and feel defeated in her ministry in China. She had hoped she and her team of missionaries would be able to bring about a revival. As time went on, nothing—*absolutely nothing*—was happening. Elsa was so discouraged she decided not to show up at a revival meeting. Noticing Elsa's absence, a fellow missionary took Elsa's motto, painted it in large letters on a sign, and hung it on the wall opposite the door to Elsa's room. That way, she couldn't avoid those words each time she entered or exited her room.

Elsa said, "When I opened the door and saw that motto hanging there—it was just too much. I went right over and turned its face to the wall. I simply couldn't for the moment bring myself to receive such a disappointment as this 'with both hands joyfully.'"[2]

Because Elsa was dwelling on what she perceived to be a lack of results, she was pretty much giving up in ministry. That's what happens when we live under our circumstances rather than above them—we feel like giving up. The pressure, whether it's physical or emotional, becomes too much for us. We become less than passionate for the things of the

Lord, feeling as if we can't go on. Our patience for answered prayer vanishes; our endurance is no more.

When we feel this way, we need to do as Elsa did. She went to Jesus for help. This was her first step out from under her circumstances. We can do the same. Jesus bids us, "Come to Me, all who are weary and heavy-laden, and I will give you rest" (Matthew 11:28).

As we lay our burdens at Jesus' feet, as we stay in communion with Him and remain content in His will, He will not only give us rest but will also make us strong: "Those who wait for the Lord will gain new strength...they will run and not get tired, they will walk and not become weary" (Isaiah 40:31).

Jesus did give Elsa rest and strength, which enabled her to carry on with her ministry and to once again believe that she could receive her difficult circumstances *joyfully with both hands*. After this lesson was learned, missionary Dr. Goforth said that Elsa had "been used mightily in all parts of China for the deepening of the spiritual life."[3]

Along with giving our burdens to Jesus, we can get above our circumstances by confronting our pain.

Confronting Our Pain

Years ago, when Brian and I lost our first child through a miscarriage, I struggled. Such a loss didn't make any sense to me. The Lord knew I had waited years for this child, and now this precious one was suddenly and unexpectedly taken from me. When I went to church that first Sunday after getting out of the hospital, I found myself sitting next to a friend who was cuddling a newborn son in her arms. I remember sitting there and asking the Lord, "Why would You allow me to sit next to this newborn when I just lost my child?" Right there, the Spirit of God showed me why. In order for me to *forget* my pain (and really stop thinking about myself), I had to *confront* my pain. What a better way to do that than to face a newborn! Strong emotions began to stir in my heart as I thanked the Lord that my friend's baby didn't lose his life in miscarriage, and that he was healthy and had an entire life ahead of him, lived out, Lord willing, for Jesus. I then began to thank the Lord that through my child I had invested in the kingdom of God. My child was now in heaven, for God's great purpose, and would be serving Him for eternity.

It's a fact: Human life is a pilgrimage, and we as travelers cannot expect to reach the end of our journey without feeling weary and worn. Life is also a voyage, and, as a result, we will encounter storms. What storm are you currently in? Or what storm have you been unable to get out of? Are you facing pain you simply cannot eliminate from your heart? How might you confront your hardship? Could you possibly reach out to someone else in that same pain? For, me this can mean reaching out to a hurting mother who has also lost a child.

If you've lost a close friend because of gossip or slander, how might you confront your situation? Having lost some dear friends myself, I have faced my pain by reaching out to women who are all alone. You can find them everywhere, especially at church. Many of them are single mothers or women married to nonbelievers. The single mothers are faced with the daunting task of raising their children by themselves, and both the single mothers and the women with nonbelieving husbands often sit alone in church. How might you reach out to these special women?

If your husband has lost his job or you've lost some precious possessions, how might you confront your pain? You could find someone less fortunate than yourself and try to reach out to her. Does your church have a food pantry you can use to help a woman in need? Occasionally the college girls I've known would end up having a broken heart because of a boyfriend breaking up with her. How do I help her face her circumstance? By encouraging her to get involved in a ministry she's interested in (or suggesting a ministry) and pouring her heart and soul into it. It works!

Ultimately, our pain and sorrow can be a blessing in disguise, if it leads us toward active compassion for others who are hurting. When we do this, we are allowing the Lord to bring about good results from our bad situation.

Even if we aren't struggling with any pain or loss, we can still reach out to the hurting with sympathy. Having sympathy for the hurting means that we share the feelings of others and we enter into the experiences of their hearts, making them our own.

Third, when it comes to getting above our circumstances, along with giving our burdens to Jesus and confronting our pain, we need to learn to accept our situation.

Accepting Our Situation

On the day of my wedding, I got up at four in the morning to spend *lots* of time with the Lord. I dove deeply in His Word and prayed more than I ever had in my life (so it seemed). I really wanted the Lord glorified on this very special day. As I prayed, I remember the Lord pressing upon my heart, "Okay, Donna, you've had your time to plan out your wedding; now it's My turn. I too have plans for this day, so trust Me if things don't go exactly how you have planned."

I remember being nervous about this prompting of the heart, but I told the Lord, "Yes, I'll accept whatever is brought to me this day." About six hours later, when I entered the bridal room at the church, one of the bridesmaids, Diana, came up to me and asked, "Have you seen the florist?"

"No, I haven't," I responded. "Isn't she here yet?"

Diana had a most unusual look on her face as she said, "Oh, she's here alright, but I'll let her speak to you!"

I thought nothing more about Diana's comment as I began getting dressed. Then, as I was putting on finishing touches of hair spray, the florist came into the room with tears running down her eyes. Crying and choking up at the same time, she exclaimed, "Your flowers...all of them...have been destroyed!"

She went on, "Yesterday had been unusually hot, so I put all the white roses for the church, your bouquet, and the bouquets for the wedding party in the freezer. They turned black!" The florist then opened her hands to show me a few of those black and very limp roses.

She then added, "I have nothing other than a few bows to decorate the church...and...well...here's a fake bouquet I've put together for you. I'm sorry it's so small. I just didn't have very many imitation roses in stock. I have nothing for the bridesmaids, groomsmen, or your parents. I tried to salvage a few roses, but the groomsmen refuse to wear them!"

At that moment, I smiled profusely. I exclaimed, "So this is what the Lord wanted me to be ready for!" What overwhelming joy I had knowing that the Hand of Providence was upon me; that He prepared me for this; and that He was moving me. As I've expressed often in this book, it is "in Him we live and move and exist" (Acts 17:28).

I then invited the florist to sit down with me on a couch and began sharing about Christ with her. What a wonderful time that was!

The florist said, "You are having too much mercy on me!"

Just then the music started playing. I looked up and I noticed the bridal room was completely empty. Barbara Ann, my maid of honor, ran in and said, "Donna, come on, you've got to get married!"

Actually, I was saddened that I had to stop talking with the florist. Grabbing for my veil and imitation flowers, I went down the aisle to start a new life with my groom. And months later, the florist received a new life with the Groom of Heaven when her sister led her to Christ. How wonderful are the words, "Truly, truly, I say to you, unless a grain of wheat falls into the earth and dies, it remains alone; *but if it dies, it bears much fruit*" (John 12:24). Yes, perhaps the "seeds" of my flowers had to die so that she could hear the gospel, and eventually receive the Lord.

So accepting our situation is key to living above our circumstances. And the best way to accept our circumstances is to *change our thinking*.

Changing Our Thinking

You are probably thinking, *How in the world c*
about my horrible trial? As tough as it is, you ca
will" rather than "I will not." There is much powe
the attitude that:

I will believe that no matter how difficult my circumstances, they
will be used for my good and the good of others who love God (Romans
8:28).

I will believe that Jesus, my Bridegroom, has an absolute, eternal love
for me (Jeremiah 31:3) and those He wishes to reach through me because
of this situation.

I will believe that my circumstance can be a catalyst God uses to help
others find Jesus.

When we have an *I will* attitude, we
take the focus off ourselves and put it
onto others. So when we are faced with
troubles, let's not get discouraged, but
learn to say with the psalmist, "Why are

> *By* not considering our
> life as so dear, we'll
> be unmoved by
> our circumstances.

you in despair, O my soul? And why are you disturbed within me? Hope
in God, for I shall again praise Him" (Psalm 43:5).

The apostle Paul had the *I will* mind-set as he faced suffering for
Christ's name's sake (see Acts 9:16). As he went "bound in spirit" to
Jerusalem, the Holy Spirit told him that in every city, "bonds and afflictions" awaited him (Acts 20:22-23). What was Paul's reply? "None of
these things move me, neither count I my life dear unto myself, so that
I might finish my course with joy" (Acts 20:24 KJV). Here Paul gives us
a great secret to embracing the joy of Christ: *not to count your life so
dear to yourself.*

By not considering our life as so dear, we'll be unmoved by our circumstances. Better than that, we'll become a godly witness to others.
As people see our confidence in God in the midst of our trials, they will

155

wn to Jesus. Of course, the devil and his demons do not want this. ey'll do whatever they can to stop you from being a witness in the midst of your difficulties. Scottish pastor Maurice Roberts made this thought-provoking statement:

> The joy of angels and Christian persons arises from their receiving news of sinners repenting and turning to God. The joy (if we may call it that) of devils springs from their witnessing anything which appears to damage the cause of God or to wound and weaken the witness of his people upon earth.[4]

It'll be more difficult for our witness to be damaged or weakened if we take one last but most important step in rising above our circumstances: keeping our focus on God.

Focusing on God

Take a look at the richest people in the world, and for the most part, you'll find an unhappy group of people. They have "everything" yet aren't satisfied. They continue to search for that "one thing" that will make them happy. Speaking to them in love, I say, "Without Jesus in your life, you'll never find true happiness and joy." As for those of us who *do* have Jesus, we also have joy, but some of us have less joy than others. Why? Because some of us get our delight from what God gives us, while those with greater joy delight *in who He is.*

The more we focus upon God, the less we are apt to focus upon our circumstances. For instance, if we have our focus on the material things that God has given us—and they are taken away—then we feel as if we are left with nothing. If we focus on *who God is*, we will never feel as if we have lost anything, even if we were stripped of all material things. What we have *in* God can never be taken from us, while what we have *from* Him can.

Let's go to Psalm 88. There we see a miserable man indeed. And it's not an exaggeration to say this person wrote one of the saddest psalms in the Bible. He goes so far as to say, "You have put me in the lowest pit" (verse 6). Yet even as bad as his situation is, he tries earnestly to redirect his attention to God. He speaks of God as being his salvation (Psalm 88:1). He dwells upon God's lovingkindness, faithfulness, wonders, and righteousness (Psalm 88:11-12). His focus upon God is what helps him pull through.

When difficult circumstances come our way, we can follow the psalmist's lead. We can begin by focusing upon God's *sovereignty*—His supreme power and authority: "Know therefore today, and take it to your heart, that the LORD, He is God in heaven above and on the earth below; there is no other" (Deuteronomy 4:39).

Let's also focus upon God's *comfort* in the midst of our affliction: "Shout for joy, O heavens! And rejoice, O earth! Break forth into joyful shouting, O mountains! For the LORD has comforted His people and will have compassion on His afflicted.... Behold, I have inscribed you on the palms of My hands" (Isaiah 49:13,16).

Let's delight in His *faithfulness*, knowing He is working in our lives, even in the midst of spiritual struggles: "God is faithful, who will not allow you to be tempted beyond what you are able, but with the temptation will provide the way of escape also, that you will be able to endure it" (1 Corinthians 10:13).

It's been said that those who know God best have the most confidence in Him. So as we continually dwell on *who* God is, we are building up greater confidence in Him—confidence that He *will* sovereignly take care of us as He did with Daniel from the power of the lions (Daniel 6:26-27). Confidence that He will be with us in our fiery furnace, comforting us, and showing compassion toward us, just as He did with Shadrach, Meshach, and Abednego (Daniel 3:25). Confidence that He *will* carry us through our trials, leading us to triumph (James 1:2-4,12).

And confidence that He *will* take us home to be with Him, either through the blessedness of death (Psalm 116:15) or the rapture (Matthew 24:30-31; 1 Corinthians 15:51-52).

Triumphing over Our Circumstances

Those of us who have Jesus have triumphed in that we are now spiritually alive in Him. And as we grow spiritually, we continue to triumph—and often, our growth comes through suffering. Those who pick up their cross as Jesus commands (Matthew 16:24) will indeed suffer hardship. Rather than suffer less than others, Christians often suffer more. In part, it's because we have a Father who disciplines us for greater spiritual growth (Hebrews 12:7-8,11). He prunes us that we "may bear more fruit" (John 15:2). It's also because "all who desire to live godly in Christ Jesus will be persecuted" (2 Timothy 3:12).

Another reason we as believers suffer more than others is because we are the devil's enemy. He desires to drag us down, especially as we are bearing much fruit, or fruit is about to come forth—such as glorifying God in various ways, leading a person to Christ, or influencing other people toward spiritual things.

We have no idea, for instance all the fruit that will be brought forth through Chris's tragic accident. When we left that story, Carolyn was at Chris's bedside, watching him struggle to stay alive and being told her own life could potentially be in danger. Carolyn was also told by the nurses that due to Chris's deep burns, he was going to look "very, very bad." Carolyn confidently responded, "We're all praying."

As Carolyn prayed earnestly for Chris and sought the Lord for comfort, she opened her Bible randomly and, amazingly, the Lord directed her to the following passage, which would sustain her:

> We have this treasure in earthen vessels, so that the surpassing greatness of the power will be of God and not

from ourselves; we are afflicted in every way, but not crushed; perplexed, but not despairing.... Therefore we do not lose heart, but though our outer man is decaying, yet our inner man is being renewed day by day. For momentary, light affliction is producing for us an eternal weight of glory far beyond all comparison, while we look not at the things which are seen, but at the things which are not seen; for the things which are seen are temporal, but the things which are not seen are eternal (2 Corinthians 4:7-8,16-18).

Yes, indeed, Carolyn and Chris were afflicted but not crushed, and perplexed but not despairing, even throughout many skins grafts and surgeries. Carolyn explains how God kept her during this time:

When going through a tremendous trial, God brings joy through small things. He makes you aware of His presence in even the smallest victories. There were bad days, but some were better by little bits of encouragement. Those moments of joy made God so real and were His way of letting me know that, even though this terrible thing had happened, He had *not* abandoned me but was with me, loved me, and cared about me.

When it was time for the bandages to come off Chris's head, Carolyn stepped out of the room and watched from a window. Observing Chris's face for the first time, Carolyn said, "Chris was all black, but still I saw his cheekbones. I was able to say to myself, 'That's still Chris there! I recognize his eyebrows. And his eyes *are still his eyes.*'"

Carolyn's prayers, and those of others, were indeed answered. Carolyn was able to see the surpassing greatness of the power of God in that Chris not only survived that horrendous ordeal, but was looking better than anyone expected. And Chris's larynx, on its own, was miraculously healed. He would be able to speak!

As Carolyn observed God's power, she wanted others to recognize it as well. For instance, the nurses were so amazed at how good Chris looked that they apologized to Carolyn for their comments. This was Carolyn's opportunity to share her conviction that "God did it!"

In a televised news conference, Carolyn said, "The doctors and nurses helped Chris tremendously, *but God was the one who performed miracles on Chris.*" Unfortunately, by the time Carolyn's statement got on the evening news, her statement crediting God was edited out.

Chris's Jewish doctor overheard what Carolyn had said, and commented, "What you said is right. Chris has had some help from the man upstairs because we can't understand why he's doing so well."

As you can see, Carolyn had *divine* joy—the only kind of joy that could possibly endure in the midst of the horrible circumstances she was experiencing. It's a joy that doesn't focus on self, but on God and others. Truly, Carolyn exemplifies the one who can say, "That I may tell of all Your praises.... I may rejoice in Your salvation" (Psalm 9:14).

When Chris returned to school two months later, he had to wear a plastic mask on his face and pressure garments (made of thick elastic) on his upper body, each for 23 hours a day for six months. To avoid the sun's rays, Chris also had to wear a wide-brim hat.

Amazingly, Chris's dramatic change in appearance has not affected him whatsoever. He said of his experience, "It wasn't the end of the world, not even close." From Chris's perspective, nothing has changed. He even wondered what the big deal was when his story was in the news.

Later on, at his high school's winter dance, Chris was elected "King of the Winter Formal." During the dance the science teacher who had asked Chris to hold the small cannon said he was sorry for what had happened that day on the field. Without an ounce of bitterness, Chris looked the teacher in the eyes and said, "I forgive you."

Enduring with Joy

Writer Edith Schaeffer and others encourage us with the words, "Don't waste your suffering." I am privileged to know several who are currently living out those words. I think of Suzy and Mike Dobreski, who experienced great sorrow when their son Benjamin died just weeks before his birth because the umbilical cord was wrapped around his neck. He went to be with the Lord while in his mother's womb. Not wanting to diminish Suzy's pain, I would like to point out how focused she and Mike have been about using their pain so that others may benefit. When their pastor approached them, he asked, "How can I help you?" The Dobreskis didn't hesitate to say, "We would like an altar call at Benjamin's funeral." And so there was an invitation for all who didn't have Jesus to receive Him. Afterward, five people committed their lives to Christ and three others requested baptism, wanting to publicly proclaim their commitment to Christ. In the midst of their pain, Suzy and Mike carried Christ's joy in their heart. As a result, Benjamin's life had quite an effect on others and will continue to do so. Only in heaven will we know the full effect of his life, and through him we are reminded that a life is better measured by impact than by duration.

I also think of my friend Margaret, who is waiting for a kidney transplant (typically about a seven-year wait), and is taking dialysis three hours a day, three days a week. Margaret explains her situation this way: "As I sit at the center undergoing treatment, I can decide to feel out of sorts, confused, and angry for the position I'm in, or I can choose to be actively searching for ways to be used by God." Because of the divine joy in Margaret, she has chosen the latter, and others are benefiting as a result.

As I write, Ed and Shelly's daughter Emily is six weeks old and battling congestive heart failure. They are also battling as they struggle over their daughter's condition. But there is still divine joy in them despite this difficult trial. Ed sent Brian and me an e-mail as he sat in the intensive care unit watching over his daughter. His note was full of joy and praise, telling us that his grandfather's heart was softening toward the things of the Lord as a result of Emily's serious condition.

While I could mention others, such as my friend Debbie who is currently (and excitedly) reaching out to others in the midst of chemotherapy, I will end with Sharon, who has a tumor in her left eye. She's had massive radiation treatments (she even had to be quarantined because she was given the highest dose allowed by the government). Complications seem to be constant. After eight major surgeries over the past three-and-a-half years, Sharon's eye problems and the pain that accompanies these problems, are not over. Her doctor, a specialist in the field, has been baffled by the constant complications and has told Sharon he feels very inadequate and frustrated.

On one occasion when Sharon was updating me on her condition, she shared with me about God's faithfulness to her and added, "I've been asking the Lord to give me an opportunity to witness to my doctor, and during the most critical time, when my doctor was most discouraged, I told him that I was thanking God for sending him into my life to care for me."

The doctor responded, "He is tormenting you!"

Sharon said, "No, He's not…He is just teaching me."

Sharon then said to me, "My heart's desire is that the doctor come to know the Lord."

Days ago, Sharon gave me another update: "My doctor and his family are going to attend the Christmas concert at church!"

What about you? Could you, in the midst of experiencing any of the situations described in this chapter, still praise Jesus and long to bring others to Him? It's a fact: People listen to the hurting. I discovered this years ago when diagnosed with a brain tumor. During those many times at the hospital taking tests, I was able to freely share Christ, and amazingly, no one squirmed—not my doctor, not the specialist, not my fellow patients in the waiting room, nor others. There was a nurse, however, who didn't appreciate the joy Jesus gave me. She asked me, in a condescending way, "You have a brain tumor! Why are you so happy?" In a word I replied, "Jesus." She didn't want to hear more. She walked away. But for the most part, people do indeed want to listen. Most of them desperately want the truth. How could they not? It's the food of the soul.[5]

It's only because of Christ's joy that any of us are able to focus on concern for others in the midst of our own difficult circumstances. Again, it's a joy that is "sorrowful yet always rejoicing" (2 Corinthians 6:10). We can rejoice in knowing that, when we are in God's will, our suffering can benefit others. Like Paul, we can talk of suffering "for your sake" (Colossians 1:24), "my tribulations on your behalf" (Ephesians 3:13) "given to me for you" (Ephesians 3:2).

This joy, so foreign to those who are not joined to Christ, can be expressed in terms of victory:

> Christ will even now, as always, be exalted in my body, whether by life or by death. For to me, to live is Christ, and to die is gain. But if I am to live on in the flesh, this will mean fruitful labor for me (Philippians 1:20-21).

Truly our joy in the midst of suffering never fails to be noticed and thereby to bear fruit. In the same way that Paul's sufferings bore fruit, our sufferings can continue to bear fruit after we are long gone.

Can you endure your cross, as Jesus, Paul, and others did? You can, and so can I, with the help of our Bridgroom, who is infinitely rich in joy which He *abundantly* bestows upon us (John 15:11)—if we choose to accept it. With this joy, He enables us to endure the unimaginable here on earth, and He inspires us to look forward to our reward in heaven:

> Behold, I am coming quickly, and My reward is with Me, to render to every man according to what he has done (Revelation 22:12).

Our Passion in Action

1. Do you have pain in your life you haven't confronted? What steps might you take to confront that pain?

2. If you are having a hard time accepting your current situation, write some "I will…" statements that will help you.

3. Read Isaiah 43:2-4. What comfort can you receive from this passage? What other verses can you meditate upon during life's difficulties?

4. What truths about God can you focus upon to help you during a difficult time?

5. How have your past or present difficulties helped someone?

6. Describe the joy of Jesus. Why is it a selfless kind of joy?

Coveting *His Love Letters*

"Your words were found and I ate them,
and Your words became for me a joy and the delight of my heart."
—JEREMIAH 15:16

Love letters are special because they express the innermost depths of the heart. For some reason, words that are difficult to say in person flow easily on a piece of paper—especially when the lovers are apart. Truly, Romeo and Juliet aren't the only ones who felt that "parting is such sweet sorrow." Sullivan Ballou certainly felt it. Sullivan, a Civil War soldier, wrote a very moving letter to his wife on July 14, 1861—just one week before his death in the Battle of First Manassas.[1] Here are some excerpts from his lengthy letter,

> My very dear Sarah:
>
> The indications are very strong that we shall move in a few days—perhaps tomorrow. Lest I should not be able to write you again, I feel impelled to write lines that may fall under your eye when I shall be no more.... Our move-ment may be one of a few days duration and full of

pleasure—and it may be one of severe conflict and death to me. Not my will, but thine O God, be done....

But, my dear wife, when I know that with my own joys I lay down nearly all of yours, and replace them in this life with cares and sorrows—when, after having eaten for long years the bitter fruit of orphanage myself, I must offer it as their only sustenance to my dear little children....

I cannot describe to you my feelings on this calm summer night, when two thousand men are sleeping around me, many of them enjoying the last, perhaps, before that of death—and I, suspicious that Death is creeping behind me with his fatal dart, am communing with God, my country, and thee.

...Sarah, my love for you is deathless, it seems to bind me to you with mighty cables that nothing but Omnipotence could break.... The memories of the blissful moments I have spent with you come creeping over me, and I feel most gratified to God and to you that I have enjoyed them so long....my dear Sarah, never forget how much I love you, and when my last breath escapes me on the battlefield, it will whisper your name.... Sarah, do not mourn me dead; think I am gone and wait for thee, for we shall meet again....[2]

That love letter, rightly so, meant so much to Sarah. It became her greatest treasure the remaining days of her life. Other women, too, during the Civil War, received precious letters from their soldiers. And those letters, too, meant everything to them. So coveted were they that many of them have been preserved and are still with us more than 140 years later.[3]

Love letters have existed since mankind could pick up a sharp rock and write a note inside a cave or on a tree. You may have received some yourself—letters that you treasure because they have special meaning to you. I've received several from Brian, but there is one that is especially written on my heart. I received it while I was in a Honduran hospital. I was very sick, very dehydrated, and in a short period of time, had gone from 103 to 83 pounds! I was disheartened and lonely, and was bedded in a drab room that had no other color but brown—brown sheets, brown ceiling, brown floor, and dark brown walls. My spirits were low both because of my surroundings and because I couldn't sleep. I had an extremely high fever, and nurses were coming in my room around the clock to slap me on the face and tell me to stay awake.

In the midst of all this, I cried out to God for help, and the Lord lovingly answered my prayer one morning when a missionary woman came rushing into my room, waving an envelope high in the air. She exclaimed, "You've got a letter from home!" It was from Brian (who was courting me at the time). I excitedly opened it up, and to my amazement, Brian expressed concern that I might get sick during my mission trip. The same had happened to him, and he encouraged me by saying that if I did get sick, I should try to keep my attitudes in check. He then included a poem that he thought would help me. Oh, what a beautiful poem it was! It spoke to my heart. What I found so amazing was that Brian had written his note to me two weeks earlier, and by the time his words finally arrived, they were perfectly timely and ministered to me tremendously. Love letters have a way of doing that.

Yet no love letter can match those written to us by God and found in the Bible. His letters are filled with *spiritual* words and expressions that people are incapable of writing, let alone thinking up. His words "are spirit and are life" (John 6:63). They reveal His heart—in fact, He Himself was the One who said, "The mouth speaks out of that which fills the heart" (Matthew 12:34). His words, then, coming from His heart, allow us to see Him. They also allow us to see Jesus. If such everlasting words have meaning to us, they will prick our heart, stir up our mind, speak to and fill up our soul.

Do your Beloved's letters have any special meaning to you? Do His letters bear life-changing power in your life? Do His thoughts and His truth help you grow more in holiness? Do His words compel an all-absorbing devotion to Him? Your answers to these questions will have much to do with what stage best describes you and your Bible reading.

The Different Stages of Bible Reading

In the past, I've struggled with making sure I spend consistent time reading my Lord's letters. I've also listened to other women share their struggles, and it seems that there are different categories of Bible readers. Some women are in the milk stage—they take just enough scriptural drink to be satisfied. Other women are in the cod-liver oil stage. They receive Scripture like medicine—they don't like the taste, but they know it is good for them. Others are in the shredded wheat stage. They regard Scripture as dry but nourishing. Then there some in the peaches-and-cream stage. They read their Beloved's love letters with great delight. They understand that His Word is the food for their soul, where the seed of spiritual passion is planted and *comes alive* as they receive communication from God.

If you find yourself in any of the first three stages, you'll be hindered in your effort to become a woman of spiritual passion. You see, your spiritual life is greatly influenced by what you feed your soul. Let's take a closer look at the different stages and see how we can put ourselves in the peaches-and-cream stage.

The Milk Stage

Without milk, newborn babies would never grow. Milk contains Vitamin B1, an essential ingredient for growth, and babies have an instinctive drive to get what they need. Likewise, spiritual newborns need spiritual milk—the very basic elements of God's Word that help them to grow. Like infants sucking at a mother's breast, spiritual babes in Christ literally long "for the pure milk of the word" (1 Peter 2:2). They can't seem to get enough of it!

Remaining Stagnant in the Word

I remember my own days as a newborn believer, of flipping through my Bible finding verses that were just so marvelous to me. I wrote down each and every verse in a journal because they were so new, so special. That's how it is when we read Scripture verses for the very first time. Truly, infancy has its delightful ways, but it's not meant to be a permanent state.

We all know that if an infant remained on milk, it would become malnourished and never grow, even if it was given plenty of Vitamin B1. Eventually the baby needs other vitamins, too. Likewise, if we stay on the milk of the Word, we too would become spiritually unhealthy. We would never grow in spiritual depth. In fact, we would…

Become Dull. When we remain satisfied to drink milk all the days of our spiritual life, we become dull—dull in our own thinking, not able to get deeper into the spiritual nourishment made available to us. Worse yet, we begin to think of God's Word as dull because we don't know how to get beyond the simple reading of verses here and there. We've gotten our fill of knowing about salvation by grace and that Jesus loves us…but is there more? Despite the supreme importance of understanding God's grace and love, if we don't get our fill with an array of spiritual food, our soul will eventually become malnourished. If we're not taking in the whole counsel of God's Word, and we're limiting our exposure to it, then it will have a limited impact on our lives. We won't see much change in us. We'll end up muting its voice to us. Imagine—if we were to "silence" the Lord in this way, we would be saying, in effect, that His Word doesn't have power to change us.

Spiritual dullness is not just a misfortune, it's a sin. It's a sin because we are neglecting to go further in the Word of God, to grow in spiritual depth. This makes it easier for worldly things to hold their grip on us. And if our eyes are fixed too much on earthly things, we'll have a hard time seeing the beauty of God's Word. If our affections remain upon the material and perishable things of this world, we will lose sight of the more important spiritual things that do not perish. Sadly, we won't be eating nourishing food, but rather, we'll be feeding "on ashes" (Isaiah 44:20) because the world is too much our focus.

Become Slow. As we continue to drink milk, our appetite won't grow. Our soul will eventually become ill-fed. This creates a *slowness in comprehending* what our Lord wants to tell us. And when we attempt to show a zeal for God before others, it won't be according to knowledge (Romans 10:2) because we won't know the Bible as well as we could. Scripture was written "that you may know" (1 John 5:13). The Bible contains the highest thoughts ever attainable, and we should set ourselves to discover, to conquer, to know it!

Become Dependent. When we remain satisfied with simply drinking milk, we stay *dependent upon others* for our spiritual growth. Instead of being passionate women who possess spiritual riches we can pass on to others, we stay as babes grasping for spiritual depth from others. Paul rebukes this type of spiritual living, saying, "For though by this time you ought to be teachers, you have need again for someone to teach you the elementary principles of the oracles of God, and you have come to need milk and not solid food" (Hebrews 5:12).

> *The* woman of spiritual passion is curious about her Beloved's letters and seeks answers to life's questions.

Become Tossed. If we never grow past the milk of the Word, we could expose ourselves to spiritual danger, being "tossed here and there by waves, and carried about by every wind of doctrine" (Ephesians 4:14). For good reason, we shouldn't stick to the milk diet for very long. Each one of us should want to mature and know more about God, His character, His plan for our lives, and how the Holy Spirit empowers and equips us for service. We ought to know not just the black and white of right and wrong, but how to discern shades of gray—how to choose the best thing from among the good things.

So how do we wean ourselves from a milk diet and move on to more substantial spiritual nourishment?

Growing Mature in the Word

Here are three general and practical steps we can take toward spiritual growth.

Step 1: Have an inquisitive mind. An inquisitive mind seeks answers for what it does not know. It searches the Scriptures. The woman of spiritual passion is curious about her Beloved's letters and seeks answers to life's questions. She also cares about her soul: "He who gets wisdom loves his own soul" (Proverbs 19:8).

Step 2: Eat meat. Decide now that you are going to start eating the meat of the Word. Choose an entire book, out of the 66 books in the Bible, that you would like to read. Decide how much you will read from that book each day—perhaps a few paragraphs? An entire chapter? Three chapters? As you carefully focus on small but whole sections of God's Word, you will absorb an array of substantial teaching. You will become more excited about the Bible because you will begin to understand its message on so many issues. And you'll understand the big picture of God's truth, rather than just bits and pieces of it from a verse here and a verse there.

Step 3: Pray. Pray to the Spirit before you read God's Word. Because we have His "anointing" (1 John 2:27), ask Him to *reveal to you* what the unbelieving eye can't see (1 John 2:27). Ask Him to help you *apply* whatever is applicable to your life.

As we take those steps, we will be doing as Scripture tells us to do—that is, growing up spiritually "in all aspects" (Ephesians 4:15).

Cod-Liver Oil Stage

For three decades now, I've taken daily a teaspoon of cod-liver oil. The benefits to the heart and skin far outweigh the ghastly taste. And yet cod-liver oil is not always beneficial, as I learned back in my college days!

Somehow I reasoned to myself that if cod-liver oil is good for me inwardly, it must be just as good for me externally. So one day while at the beach, I smothered myself with cod-liver oil. When it was time for me to leave and get ready for a first-time date, I stopped by the store. My friend Janet saw me and said, "Donna, you smell just like a fish! What have you been doing?" I told Janet what I had done and said, "It's no big deal. I'm going home to clean up."

I took a long, hot shower and scrubbed "the tar" out of my skin. Just as I was putting on the finishing touches of makeup, my roommate Joyce came home from work. She came right up to me and said, "Donna, you smell just like fish! Your hair, your skin, your clothes...you smell awful!"

Even though I had thoroughly washed the cod-liver oil from my skin, it apparently had marinated my pores and was even affecting my beautiful new dress. I simply couldn't get rid of the smell. Unfortunately, it was too late to call Jerry to cancel our date. He would be arriving at the apartment any minute. So I decided to try a fresh-air ruse by waiting for him outside. I lived right on the beach, and I figured the salt air would easily hide the smell.

When Jerry came by to pick me up, I quickly jumped in his car and rolled down my window—*all the way down!* Driving along the shoreline, Jerry exclaimed, "Boy, you sure can smell the fish tonight! It stinks!"

Not knowing what to say, I kept silent and just nodded my head in agreement.

When we got to the restaurant, I was glad it was right on the shore. Jerry ordered steak, and I bet you can guess what I ordered—fish! While I was eating my fillet (which wasn't very appetizing, considering the circumstances), Jerry talked about having lived on the beach all his life and that "I don't ever recall it smelling so bad!" He even said that the horrible oil spill a few years earlier, and the subsequent smell from all the dead fish—didn't smell as bad as it did right now.

All I wanted to do was go home and cover myself with oatmeal, or anything else for that matter, to get rid of that smell! After dinner, Jerry drove me home. I quickly thanked him for the "wonderful time," jumped out of the car, and ran inside my apartment as fast as I could. Jerry never did call me afterward. I'm sure he must have thought there was something *very* "fishy" about me.

I had put cod-liver oil all over my skin because of my mistaken assumption that using it externally might be good. But my idea backfired on me, causing me to smell like a three-week-old strike in a fish cannery. Likewise, when we take a cod-liver oil approach to our Bible reading, in which we read only because "it's good for us" and nothing more than that, we too can end up smelling pretty fishy, spiritually. While we may be entertaining thoughts about God as we read the Scriptures, good thoughts aren't enough when they aren't penetrating the heart. We must *love* the things of God in order to understand them, in order for them to affect us, and in order to enhance our spiritual passion.

Loving the Divine Word

How can we get past the "it's good for us" way of thinking, and develop a true love for the Word? It's the Holy Spirit who enlightens us to understand and apply God's Word, and we need to be dependent on His guidance:

> Things which eye has not seen and ear has not heard, and which have not entered the heart of man, all that God has prepared for those who love Him. For to us God revealed them *through the Spirit;* for the Spirit searches all things, even the depths of God....the thoughts of God no one knows except the Spirit of God (1 Corinthians 2:9-12).

Because the Spirit knows the thoughts of God, He can guide us in the Word like no other. I remember one day, when I had felt so far from the Word, the Spirit picked me up and eased me back into it. I'll never forget His approach. He simply prompted me to pick up the Bible and begin an odyssey of skimming through its pages, going from Genesis through Revelation. In this adventure, I came to see that the Bible is much more than simply an account of nations, wars, and commands—it is about individuals very much like you and me.

The champions of Scripture did not live in a utopia, nor were they on some misty level of sainthood. They lived under many of the same conditions we live under today, struggling against evil within their very souls. We can read about them in their homes, at work, in love, at a marriage feast, at a funeral. There are those we can read about who stumbled in their spiritual life and became more prone to temptation (see footnote 4 for examples found on page 237). They indeed showed their humanness, and because of their errors, we can learn a great deal from them. But too, we can learn from the lives of those with a spiritual passion whose faith showed great results—*such people can inspire and motivate us* (see footnote 5 for examples found on page 237). When we remember that the victorious saints actually lived in history and were subject to the same temptations we are, we realize that the passion they had for the things of God is within our own reach. The trials they endured we too can endure; the eternal perspective that guided them can also guide us. The story that transformed their lives can also transform ours. After all, we have the same Spirit to strengthen us, and the same Spirit to "teach us concerning His ways" (Isaiah 2:3).

Jesus said of the Holy Spirit, "He will guide you into all the truth" (John 16:13). Truly, it is God's Word that teaches us, guides us, and detects the true spiritual condition of our soul. It penetrates our innermost thoughts and desires. But that penetration comes *only* when we read the Word not because we "have to," not because "it's good for us," but because we earnestly desire that it transforms us. That desire comes to us from the Spirit. *Just ask Him for that desire, and He'll give it to you.* He will help you understand Scripture's teachings in light of your own experiences—your joys, sorrows, and needs. And one key way to allow the Spirit to meet your deep spiritual longings is by making a habit of setting aside a regular time for devotional reading of the Word. By the way, the Psalms are a wonderful book in which to begin your devotional reading. Here we find almost every type of human emotion and experience brought into relation with God. The Psalms have a way of prompting us to pray with the psalmist for a renewed passion for God and His Word.

Does your passion for God's Word match that of the psalmist? Consider what he says:

> I cried with all my heart; answer, O LORD! I will observe Your statutes. I cried to You; save me and I shall keep Your testimonies. I rise before dawn and cry for help; I wait for Your words. My eyes anticipate the night watches, that I may meditate on Your word. Hear my voice according to Your lovingkindness; revive me, O LORD, according to Your ordinances (Psalm 119:145-149).

Cultivating the Right Attitude

Gaining this kind of enthusiasm and love for the Bible is not so much a technique as it is an attitude. Dr. Merrill Tenney, former dean of Wheaton Graduate School, says, "It is the spirit of eagerness which seeks the mind of God; it is the spirit of humility which listens readily to the voice of God; it is the spirit of adventure which pursues earnestly the will of God; it is the spirit of adoration which rests in the presence of God."[6]

> Our spiritual passion has so much to do with our involvement in God's Word.

When we go through those periods of feeling as if the Word of God isn't alive to us, we need to remember there are *two* entities in this equation: the Holy Spirit and ourselves. We can always be sure the Spirit is actively working on our behalf. But we know there are times when we're not putting forth any effort. Only when we make a genuine effort to spend time in the Word can we "press on to know the LORD" (Hosea 6:3) and grow in the knowledge of God, the thoughts of God, the ways of God, the pleasures of God, the will of God.

Our spiritual passion has so much to do with our involvement in God's Word. And while our devotional reading should not be measured by the clock, it is true that the more time we put into it, the more we will get out of it.

One thing I have found that makes God's Word even closer to my heart is to make it as personal as possible by putting myself into its pages.

Putting Ourselves into the Pages of Scripture

Let's go back in time and put ourselves in Scripture's pages. Let's make this adventure as vivid as possible, trying to know what it would be like to see what the people of the Bible saw, heard, and felt. Let's, for instance, go to what appears to be a gloomy scene. Christ has been buried, and

His followers are devastated and disillusioned. Imagine yourself as part of this group of grieving individuals. Then go with Mary Magdalene in the darkness of early morning and observe that the stone guarding Jesus' grave was moved. What questions arise in your mind? Mary believed that Christ's body had been stolen. How would it feel to think that the Lord, whom you loved so much, had had his body stolen? What would the thieves have done with it? Might they have thrown the body down some remote cliff?

Filled with anxiety, you and Mary run to tell the disciples. You both see Peter and John, and approach them. While you catch your breath, Mary exclaims, "They have taken away the Lord out of the tomb, and we do not know where they have laid Him" (John 20:2). You all run back to the tomb.

The disciples see the linen wrappings and face cloth still present within the tomb, but they are still quite puzzled, "for as yet they did not understand the Scripture, that He must rise again from the dead" (John 20:9). Peter and John are discouraged and decide to walk back home, while you and Mary stay, standing outside the tomb, weeping. Stooping again to look inside the tomb, you wonder, *What could have become of the body?*

While your thoughts vacillate between puzzlement and grief, you are startled by two figures who appear before you. They are clothed in white, with "one at the head and one at the feet, where the body of Jesus had been lying" (verse 12). They gently ask you and Mary, "Why are you weeping?" (verse 13).

Mary answers, "They have taken away my Lord, and I do not know where they have laid Him" (verse 13).

You both turn around and see a man standing right behind you. Thinking he is the gardener, Mary asks if he took away her Lord's body. And if so, she'll recover it (verse 15). You, too, want to help Mary recover the body.

Suddenly, all your concerns melt away in astonishment. Sorrow turns instantly to joy, sadness to jubilee. Why? Because you hear the man, whom you thought was the gardener, call you by name—He knows you, and you know Him. It is the risen Lord! (verse 16).

Can you see the difference in perspective that we gain when we put ourselves in the biblical narrative? By such a practice, we can imagine, in greater depth, the thoughts that might have crossed the minds of the people in the Bible, and feel their joy and anguish. We can imagine, for example, Peter's mixed feelings upon seeing the risen Lord after he had boasted, "Lord, with You I am ready to go both to prison and to death!" (Luke 22:33). As we know, Peter's confidence withered when people confronted him as one of the disciples (Luke 22:54-62). We can also well imagine that Peter might have had his three denials in mind when he wrote in his epistle that we need to humble ourselves (1 Peter 5:6). Also, do you remember, shortly before the crucifixion, Jesus' admonishment to Peter, "Simon, Simon, behold, Satan has demanded permission to sift you like wheat" (Luke 22:31)? Could it be that Peter was remembering that very admonishment when he wrote that we should beware of our spiritual adversary, who is constantly looking for someone to destroy (1 Peter 5:8)?

Understanding the Themes of the Bible

A wonderful way to grow in God's Word is to understand the major themes of the Bible. Then when we are in need of immediate help, we can know exactly where our Lord addressed our need. We can use this information to help others, too. For instance, are we or someone else suffering injustice while it seems as if God is doing nothing? To find comfort and understanding as to what God may be doing, we can turn to the book of Habakkuk.

Does a Jewish friend need to understand who the Messiah is? A good place to start is to take her to the book of Isaiah (especially chapter 53).

As we know, Jewish people only recognize the Old Testament, so it's important to build bridges with what they respect. When they become more open to truth, they'll be willing to listen to truth from the New Testament. While we can point to Jesus "beginning with Moses and with all the prophets" (Luke 24:27), the book of Isaiah deals with the person and work of Christ more than any other book in the Old Testament.

Do you have a friend who is listening to false teachers? Have her read Jude and 2 Peter.

Do you or a friend need a better grasp of God's grace in salvation? Ephesians (especially 2:8-9) and Romans are the books to read.

By better grasping the entire range of Scripture, we can get the full counsel of God and be equipped to help ourselves and others. Let's take a quick trip, going back in time, to get a better sense of what each book, written for our instruction and benefit, is about.

Going back in time to *Genesis*, we behold
the beginning of mankind—for centuries it's been told.
There we see beauty in the image of God
but also a horrific darkness—who would have thought?
Cast out of the Garden because of the sinning,
we go to *Exodus* and encounter plagues oh so chilling!

In *Leviticus*, which means, "He is called,"
we hear God's command to holiness for us all.
In *Numbers* we live with the Jews in the wilderness,
in *Deuteronomy* Moses' last words, of tenderness.
Joshua tells us of conquest and division,
of a land overflowing with God's provision.
In *Judges* we see conquest and monarchy,
and *Ruth* stands out with love and charity.

Go to *First Samuel*—every child's delight,
and watch in suspense David and Goliath's fight.
On to *Second Samuel,* David's reign and victories,
but also the sin that brought him his miseries.

Next it's *First* and *Second Kings,* originally one book,
and the history of the monarchy—an exciting look!
First Chronicles means "the affairs of the day"
and there we get a glimpse of King David's praise.
Second Chronicles teaches us to be humble and pray,
to seek God's face, and turn from wicked ways.

Ezra fills us with memoirs and family trees,
while *Nehemiah* gives us the history of Babylonian refugees.
Esther and *Job* show how God controls all events.
But, too, lest we forget, Job's friends say, "Repent!"
Dwelling in the *Psalms,* we hear laments and praises,
and *Proverbs* supplies us with wisdom for all ages.
Visiting *Ecclesiastes,* we see life's puzzling paradoxes,
while *Song of Solomon* shows
how to protect marital love from "foxes."

Be awed as *Isaiah* prophesies Christ the Messiah, the God-sent.
Be solemn as *Jeremiah* warns us against sin and judgment.
Lamentations, a Greek verb, meaning "to cry aloud,"
describes for us Jerusalem's destructive dark cloud.
Ezekiel, "God Strengthens," his name is called,
speaks of remembrance of sin and restoration to all.

Daniel you remember, being in the lion's den,
shows God's faithfulness to his three friends.
Hosea, a prophet, reveals God's steadfast love,
and *Joel* speaks of deliverance coming from above.
Take heed to *Amos* as he confronts
the evils of the day,
While *Obadiah* speaks of Edom's doom
because of its evil ways.

Spend time with *Jonah* in the belly of a fish,
then watch him preach to the Ninevites—against his wish!
Listen to *Micah's* message, loud and clear,
each key section starts with the word, "Hear."
Nahum describes for us a God who's strong,

while *Habakkuk* questions, "Oh Lord, how long?"
Zephaniah speaks of judgment as his major theme,
and *Haggai* desires righteous living that is supreme.
Zechariah talks of hope and the return of Christ,
while *Malachi* confronts ungodliness as a blight.

Matthew pronounces Christ as the King of kings.
Mark speaks of Christ as a servant—love He brings.
Luke shows us the Lord Christ as the "Son of Man,"
while *John* articulates Christ's miracles, not His life-span.

Jump into *Acts* for action and suspense,
the start of the church, the Spirit's entrance.
In *Romans* a number of doctrines are discussed
and, foremost of them all, Christ's relationship with us.
In *First Corinthians* Paul confronts Christians who are sinning;
in *Second Corinthians* he presents the principles for giving.

Be excited in *Galatians*—and believe, we must—
that we are crucified with Christ, and He lives in us!
Just as wonderful, in *Ephesians*, we are given more than a perk,
we learn the way to heaven is by grace and not work.

Over in *Philippians* we follow Christ's example,
and in *Colossians*, His all-sufficiency is ample.
First Thessalonians describes for us events of the last days,
while *Second Thessalonians* centers on man's evil ways.
Listen as *First Timothy* tells us to "fight the good fight,"
While *Second Timothy* calls us to "be a good soldier of Christ."

Meet *Titus*, a man who received Paul's letter
to pass on the message of qualifications for elders.
Philemon, a letter from Paul while in prison
pleas for Christian brotherhood—and with good reason.
Hebrews tells the stories of those who lived with great faith,
and how with confidence we can go to the throne of His grace.

James tells how faith works in everyday life
First Peter exhorts every believer in Christ.

Second Peter, with concern, denounces all false teachers
who would try, if they could, to deceive all true seekers.

First John is a book filled with all kinds of contrasts:
light and darkness; love and hate; eternal life and outcasts.
Second John's message about walking in truth and love,
means stay away from deceivers regarding spiritual things above.
Third John, like First and Second, tells how we should
remember to imitate that which is good.

Jude is a book as short as can be,
warning about false teachers, exhorting you and me.
Revelation, the last book we visit in the Bible
speaks of Christ's return and a gigantic revival!

Now that we've been through the Bible today,
We've seen the truth of God on display.
To us did He give His Word from above,
that we may have a passion—to reveal His love.[7]
—D.M.

A passion that reveals His love—that's what I want for my life. But I know I won't have such passion unless I continue to hunger more and more for His Word. And I need to eliminate those hindrances that keep me from the peaches-and-cream stage.

The Shredded Wheat Stage

One day I saw on the Internet a chat room in which recipes were exchanged. One woman mentioned Spoon-Size Shredded Wheat and using this cereal as a snack. She said,

> I tried them plain…and they taste pretty good (like Triscuits) but they're really dry. I thought they might be good if I baked them with some kind of seasoning (maybe soy sauce?). I was wondering if anyone on the list had ever tried anything like this and could share the results.[8]

The woman made that comment back in 1997, and years later her question is still on the Internet, begging for an answer. Shredded wheat, I discovered, is a hot topic on the Internet, with people looking for ways to use it. There is a chain of craft stores that recommends you use shredded wheat for your Christmas Nativity scenes. Crush it up, and it'll look just like straw.[9]

You may or may not be interested in learning about the ways shredded wheat can be used, but you do want to make sure you're not in the shredded-wheat stage in relation to Scripture reading—dry, but nourishing. For those of us in this stage, we want to get rid of the "dryness," like the woman who was searching for ideas in the exchange on the Internet.

Recipe for Getting Rid of the Dryness

Let's first ask the obvious: "Is it God's Word that is dry, or is it we?" When we read the Bible, we are reading words that come from the breath of our Lord's very lips. So it's a Word that's very much alive. If there's any dryness, it's from us. And to get rid of the "dryness" in our Bible study, we must go back to what drew us to the Word of God in the first place.

As we know, our memory stores what it desires, what it's concerned about, and what affects us. God's deeds affected one psalmist in such a way that he proclaimed, "I shall remember the deeds of the LORD; surely I will remember Your wonders of old" (Psalm 77:11). Another psalmist affected by the days of the past said, "I remember the days of old; I meditate on all Your doings" (Psalm 143:5). As these two psalmists reflected on their memories of God's great work, they got excited. There were specific events or truths that, in their minds, led them to long for God and spurred special feelings in their hearts.

If you are in the dry stage, may I ask, Do you remember what it was about God's Word that used to excite you? What events and truths in the Lord's love letters have you cherished most?

Where is the blessedness I knew
When first I saw the Lord?
Where is the soul-refreshing view
Of Jesus and His Word?

What peaceful hours I once enjoyed!
How sweet their memory still!
But they have left an aching void
The world can never fill.[10]

When we begin to remember those cherished moments we had with the Lord and His Word, we will find ourselves saying, "Revive me according to Your word" (Psalm 119:25 NKJV). Yes! That's what we need—revival! Revival that will get rid of our dryness.

Need for Spiritual Revival

Let's go back to when Christ was alive. The chief religious leaders and scribes wanted to destroy Him. But for a while, they couldn't touch Him. That's because "all the people were hanging on to every word He said" (Luke 19:48). They were in complete amazement over His teachings, and He was immensely popular with the masses.

Just as the crowds were excited about every word that proceeded from the mouth of God, we too can have the same passion for His words. We can ask Him to bring His teaching alive to us and revive our soul: "Great are Thy mercies, O LORD; *revive me* according to Your ordinances" (Psalm 119:156). Note that it's His *ordinances*—His teachings—that can revive our heart.

Revival allows us to once again experience the Spirit's illuminating of our minds, showing us the mysteries of His Word, and giving us, in the same way that Christ gave the Emmaus disciples, *new insight* (Luke 24:31), *new energy* (Luke 24:32-35), and a *natural desire to share with others what we've learned from the Word* (Luke 24:35). As Christ spoke to these men on the road to Emmaus, they felt their hearts burning within them (Luke 24:32). And we can ask the Lord to let His own words revive us similarly.

Does revival seem difficult to you this moment? Does it seem hard because you've lived in the land of dryness for some time? Do you feel as though you've exhausted the Scriptures, that there is nothing new for you to learn?

No matter how familiar you are with your Beloved's Word, you can still learn new truths as you search out the Bible's less-trodden paths and its hidden nooks and crannies. There's always so much more that is hidden beneath the sound of familiar words and phrases which, from frequent hearing or repetition, may have lost their power in getting our attention.

Let's see if we can turn all this around and look closer at the familiar to find something new and exciting. In fact, you will notice that when you *want* to get more out of God's Word, you *will* get more. It's a matter of purposely looking at Scripture with a desire to discover and learn.

Appreciating the Familiar

Let's see if we can look at the familiar and appreciate it in a new way. For example, what was the very first thing God told us in His love letter to us? You and I know the answer, but it's become *so familiar* to us that we probably can't give the answer right away. Give up? He wrote that He created heaven (Genesis 1:1). That is the very first statement He made, and it's the first thing He gave for us to think about. And the knowledge of what awaits us in heaven gives us something to hope for, to cheer us, to sustain our soul.

Here's another example—the simple words, "It is written" (Matthew 4:4,7,10). These three little words, on their own, hardly offer any meaning to us. But in context, we see that it was those very words that became threatening to the devil. They became the very sword of the Spirit that baffled and vanquished him from the presence of Jesus. When Jesus quoted what was written, He did so because He knew that God's Word, in and of itself, has power. God's truth can have an impact—particularly on how we live. Not only can it send Satan scurrying away, but also it can give us encouragement and help for the very real problems of everyday life.

With God's Word in hand, you have access to divine power! Far from the Word being dry, it can be the most valuable tool you have, especially when you are being bothered by the devil. You can do just as Jesus did. You can remind Satan, "It is written," and then cite a verse that rebukes whatever lie Satan is telling you. Combating the devil with Scripture is a sure way to get rid of him!

Now that we've seen the hindrances to growth in God's Word, we're ready to talk about the peaches-and-cream stage—that blessed place in our spiritual life where reading the Scriptures is our greatest delight.

Peaches-and-Cream Stage

I love the book of Nehemiah and the very dear people in this book—the remnant of Jews who survived captivity, distress, and reproach while in Babylon. They were a hurting people, and when Nehemiah heard their sad story, he wept and mourned for days (Nehemiah 1:4).

Despite all they had been through, these people *loved the Word of God*. So much so that they wept when they heard it (Nehemiah 8:9). The Word also prompted them to confess, worship, pray, and offer thanksgiving (Nehemiah 9:3-38). These people appreciated the Word of God so much because while they were captives, the Word wasn't readily available to them. Now that they were free, they were thirsty for it. They couldn't get enough of it.

It's been said that we do not grieve over what we do not value. If we no longer had access to God's Word, would we value it more? Would we crave it more? Would we relish it once we got it back? This is what God wants. He wants us to appreciate His Word.

Consider what God told Joshua about His Word: "Do not turn from it to the right or to the left" (Joshua 1:7). God told Joshua to "meditate on it day and night, so that you may be careful to do according to all that is written in it" (Joshua 1:8).

Our dear Lord wants the same for us, too. He wants us to indulge in His Word and meditate upon it. Why meditate? Because meditation—that is, a concentrated and thoughtful mulling over something over a period of time—helps information to truly permeate into the depths of our hearts and minds.

The Value of Biblical Meditation

When I read Psalm 119, I am in awe over the fact the psalmist knew *so much* about the Word of God. Can you guess as to why the psalmist was able to write so eloquently about God's precepts? Because he meditated upon God's Word (see Psalm 119:15, 23, 48, 78, 97). He knew God's truth better because he thought so much about it.

When any of us read the Bible, we will come to *know* about God and His truth. But when we meditate upon it, we will know *much more* about God and what He has to say. Imagine two tourists visiting the Louvre, the famous art museum in France. The first tourist passes by each painting fairly quickly, getting no more than general impressions. The second tourist stops at each painting and spends plenty of time observing each one closely. She pays close attention to people's expressions, the colors of various objects, the backgrounds, and so on. She even ponders the painter's intent and the message he or she is trying to communicate. Which one of the tourists is going to know more about the paintings upon leaving the museum?

This is what meditation is all about—it's paying close attention to what's in front of us as we read our Beloved's love letters. It's pondering over the heavenly words rather than skimming over them.

With this in mind, let's look at some ways we can become more skilled at mediating upon God's Word.

The Elements of Biblical Meditation

Step 1: Give yourself some time. It's a fact: We need *time* to quietly bring our thoughts heavenward. This is hard because we are living in a day and age where we are constantly preoccupied, where distractions are many, where every hour is taken up with tasks to do. Let us not allow the things of this world to take us away from meditating upon words that came from the throne of God. Set some time aside. Try somehow to work it into your schedule, whether in the morning, afternoon, or evening.

Step 2: Ask questions. In a high school journalism class, I learned that a great way to seek understanding of an event or a written work is to ask six basic questions: Who? What? When? Where? Why? And how? As we ask these questions in response to what we read in Scripture, we will notice the key facts becoming much more apparent, and thus get a clearer understanding of what's going on in the text we are reading.

Step 3: Paraphrase. After reading a Scripture passage, explain to yourself, in your own words, what is being said to you.

Step 4: Pray. Ask the Lord to help you dwell upon His message throughout the day. Ask Him to help you apply what you have read to your life.

To get a better idea of what biblical meditation looks like, let's read 1 Peter 5:1-11 and go through the steps we just learned.

The Practice of Biblical Meditation

After reading 1 Peter 5:1-11, *Ask:*

Who is Peter speaking to? The elders and other church leaders.

What is the message? By looking at the key words, we can see this text is about living a life of *humility, casting* your anxiety upon the Lord, and being on the *alert* for the evil one.

When are these leaders to act upon Peter's instructions? Now and always.

Why was this message written? There may have been some leadership problems in the church, and possibly some selfish ambitions—otherwise Peter would not have told them *how* they were to "*shepherd* the flock of God…*not* under compulsion, but voluntarily…*not* for sordid gain, but with eagerness; *nor* yet as lording it over those allotted to your charge, but proving to be examples to the flock" (verses 2-3).

Paraphrase: In my own words, I see this chapter is telling leaders in the church that they need to really take care of the flock. And to do it properly, they must have humility. Being shepherds of the church, they are continually helping others—but who is helping them? Jesus, who sees all, realizes they need someone, so He offers Himself to them, telling them to give all their anxiety to Him. So too must we (Matthew 11:24). But, there is a warning for the elders as well. If they don't give the Lord their concerns, the devil is ready to devour them (1 Peter 5:7-8). The enemy hates what they are doing. Therefore, dependence upon the Lord is their only hope for deliverance from the evil one.

Pray. Dear Lord, help me this day [or evening] to dwell upon and apply what I have just read from Your Word. Though I am not a leader in the church, I know I could become a more godly woman by applying this same message to myself and giving You all my anxieties. Help me to be a humble woman—do whatever You need to in my life so I can become just that. And help me to give You all my anxieties [list the concerns that you want to surrender to Him]. Help me to leave *everything* in Your Hands so that I will not live a life of worry. Amen.

A Final Thought

Our Beloved's love letters to us, His bride, were written that we may draw closer to Him, know Him better, feel His very heart beating with affection for us, and to feed our soul: "Your words were found and I ate them, and Your words became for me a joy and the delight of my heart" (Jeremiah 15:16).

As an expression of our love, we can communicate daily with Him, giving thanksgiving and praise to our Bridegroom in response to what we've learned. It will take us an entire lifetime to respond to all that He has written down for us. And especially exciting is the fact that someday we will see Him face to face and can tell Him, "I read and meditated upon all that You told me. I cherished Your truths in my heart. Now I am here to sit at Your feet and to listen to You even more!"

> The Spirit and the bride say, "Come."
> And let the one who hears say, "Come."
> And let the one who is thirsty come....
> —Revelation 22:17

Our Passion in Action

1. Recount a time when the Lord's Word really excited you. What was it about His love letters that you cherished most?

2. Write in a notebook the Scripture verses that are most meaningful to you. Why are these verses so special?

3. Practice biblical meditation: To sharpen your biblical meditation skills, go through the steps Ask, Paraphrase, and Pray as you read each of the following verses. What does the Bible tell you about...

   —spiritual feasting (Jeremiah 15:16)?

   —spiritual dressing (Ephesians 4:22-24)?

   —our spiritual dwelling (Psalm 27:4)?

4. If you were to attempt to explain to an unbeliever why the Word of God wasn't dry, dull, or a boring book, what would you say?

10

Telling Others I Am His, He Is Mine

"My beloved is mine, and I am his."
—SONG OF SOLOMON 2:16

I grew up in a home with four brothers and one sister, and many of their friends became my friends. One of those friends was George, who was like another brother to me. I remember many nice qualities about George, especially his kindness, which was appreciated by everyone who got to know him. We enjoyed each other's company as we grew up, and eventually it was time to say good-bye when he went off to college. A few years later, I too left town, and we lost contact with one another.

Close to ten years later, while at a church far from where we grew up, I heard someone excitedly calling out my name. It was George! He was thrilled to see that I had become a Christian. I was thrilled to find out that he was a Christian as well, and I asked him, "When did you accept Christ?"

George's face turned red as he said, "When I was about ten."

You can probably guess what I said next: "George, why didn't you ever tell me about Jesus?"

George turned many more shades of red. He was silent for a moment and looked all around as if he wanted to find a way of escape. After a few awkward moments, he explained, "Donna, words can't express how sorry I am that I never told you about Him, or my commitment to Christ. I was too intimidated; I succumbed to peer pressure. I...I...I was spiritually weak. I feared I would lose your friendship. Can you forgive me?"

Certainly I forgave George. I wonder how many people I myself should be seeking forgiveness from for not telling them about our wonderful Lord!

As Christians, we are married to the Groom of heaven. What kind of relationship do we have with Him? Do we have a closet marriage, where we keep our commitment to Him a secret? I'm sure that we would *never* consider keeping our relationship with Jesus a secret. But, let's go one step further. Do we go out of our way to let others know about our relationship with Him? Or do we just wait for people to ask?

Sometimes we are quiet about our love relationship with Jesus because we fear the reaction we might get from others. The best way to change this is to first understand the conflict that we face, and then second, come to the realization that those without Jesus will indeed face horror if they don't become saved.

Understanding the Conflict

Today, just as in John the Baptist's day, society judges all human beings—including Christians—by worldly standards. According to those standards, we who are believers may be regarded as crazy extremists, right-wing zealots, fundamentalists, or religious nuts.[1] Those who oppose us prefer that we try to please them and accommodate their standards with regard to such things as fashion, the tolerance of evil, and our stance on social issues. Those who aren't Christians don't like it when we talk about right and wrong or absolute truth. Look at what happened to Jason and other Christians after they forthrightly expressed their opinion—they were dragged before the city authorities because they had "upset the world" (Acts 17:6).

Of course, those Christians didn't literally upset the world. Rather, they had upset those who had an opposition to the truth of Jesus Christ, those who were proud and self-centered. Those who pursued the arts, philosophy, science, literature, and intellectual attainments while mocking God. That was the world Jason and his Christian friends had upset. And our world hasn't changed one bit since.

Look at Thomas Paine (1737–1809), the skeptic and American revolutionary. He not only had a fanatical opposition to the truth of Jesus Christ, but also toward Christians in general. Referring to the Lord's command to turn the other cheek, he said that Christians have the "spirit of a spaniel."[2] As he saw it, turning the other cheek destroys our proper self-respect. So too does loving one's enemy. He said such dogma was a make-believe morality and has no meaning.[3]

Comments such as his shouldn't surprise us too much. However, our tendency when we hear negative statements about Christianity is to just nod our head, as if in agreement, or simply be quiet and not show the unbeliever what is wrong with her thinking. It's so much easier to simply "get along" and keep the peace. Yet we shouldn't let our desire for peace with others make us fearful about standing up for our beliefs. If we're not careful, we could end up becoming more guided by the world's convictions rather than those of Jesus—all because we want to be accepted.

If our tendency is to cave in to the pressure of others and keep quiet about our relationship with Jesus in order to keep the peace, then we need to radically change our thinking. How? *By thinking about the eternal destiny of those who are spiritually lost.* It's when we come to really understand what eternity could hold for an individual that we begin to reach out.

Thinking About What Awaits the Lost

Have you walked through a graveyard lately? A few years ago I made a memorable visit to a cemetery where my grandfather is buried. As I strolled over the grassy hills, I reflected on memories of the people I knew who now silently lay there. I enjoyed standing at my grandfather's grave and thought about how, at the age of 90, he surrendered his life to Jesus.

Leaving my grandfather, I visited other tombstones, one of which memorialized a woman we'll call Betty. When Betty was alive, she opposed my wedded life to Jesus Christ. She had known me since childhood and didn't like seeing me become so "religious." There were times when Betty would scream at me or hang up the phone on me. On one occasion she kicked me out of her house in pouring rain, not even letting me back in to get my raincoat. Often she would not speak to me for months at a time—all because I would mention the name *Jesus*.

As I looked at her grave, I wondered, *Where is Betty now? Was this sick world the only heaven she knew?*

My last opportunity to share with Betty was at her deathbed. Her family called to tell me she was in the hospital. I drove a few hours' distance to go see her. When I walked into her room, we were alone, and Betty was in a coma. At least she was still alive. I stood there, filled with great emotion, wondering if the Lord would allow Betty to even have a "deathbed experience." Very few people have such an experience, and not one of us can dare trust ourselves to a hope so slender. Even so, I was hoping this for Betty. I prayed, "Please, dear Jesus, awaken Betty!" I put my hands around her arm, squeezed it as tightly as possible, and said firmly, "Betty! Betty! Betty!"

Betty came out of the coma, which she had been in for days. She began spitting up quite a bit of blood. Her fear-filled eyes and my teary eyes met. She said with great effort, "I'm in so much pain!"

I pleaded, "Betty, give your pain to Jesus. Ask Him to forgive you of your sins and to have mercy on your soul! You have only a few hours left before you enter into eternity. Ask Him to receive you into His kingdom."

Again she repeated, "But I'm in so much pain!"

I pleaded, "Betty, give your pain to Jesus! Give Him everything—your pain, your life, your sins. Seek His forgiveness, and ask Jesus to have mercy on your soul! Would you like me to assist you in praying to Him?"

As soon as I said those words, Betty slipped back into her coma. My hope is that Betty was able to cry out to God, even in her coma. She died a few hours later, and when she did, her destiny was in God's hands.

> *B*oldness thinks about Jesus and calls up the courage to share with others out of a concern for their eternal destiny.

Sometimes I can't help but think, *What if Betty isn't with Jesus? And, if not, what is she experiencing this very moment?* While I was standing at her grave, I tried to imagine what she might be experiencing (yet it's impossible for us to really know—I agree with the view that people will suffer varying amounts of punishment in hell[4]). Do you ever imagine what the eternally lost are experiencing? For many people who are now dead, hell became a truth discovered too late. There is *nothing* that they, who are in a Christless eternity, can do to better their situation (Hebrews 9:27). And contrary to popular opinion, they aren't resting in peace. They are weeping and gnashing their teeth (Matthew 8:12).

Have you ever read Nathaniel Hathorne's nineteenth-century story *The Celestial Railroad*? Everyone aboard the train is comfortably seated, believing they're on their way to the Celestial City, but in reality they are on their way to the City of Destruction. Horrible story, isn't it? Hawthorne ends his story with the relief that it was only a dream…but in real life, for many people, it won't be a dream. This unexpected surprise is going to be a reality for many people who are currently living among us. What helps me build a spiritual passion to reach the lost is to picture those whom I know at the Great White Throne, awaiting Christ's judgment (Revelation 20:11). I imagine myself standing at

Christ's side as He condemns for eternity someone whom I should have reached out to. I see their pitiful faces, looking at me in horror, and asking what I asked George: "Why didn't you ever tell me?"

Fortunately, we can tell people about Jesus *now* before it's too late. Our gratitude for Christ's forgiveness of our sins should be so great that "we cannot stop speaking about what we have seen and heard" (Acts 4:20). Have you ever considered the fact that you are "read by all men...you are a letter of Christ...written not with ink but with the Spirit of the living God, not on tables of stone, but on tablets of human hearts" (2 Corinthians 3:2-3)? You are a "Christ-letter" who has Christ's divine thoughts stamped on your heart—thoughts to be read by those who are unwilling to read a Bible. It's a Christ-letter intended to stir up the soul of others.

> Jesus, confirm my heart's desire,
> to communicate Your thoughts through me:
> Instill in me Your holy fire,
> stirring up souls for Thee!
> —D.M.

Stirring Up the Souls of Others

You might be wondering, *How can I stir up the souls of others?* By taking the thoughts of God and communicating them with boldness. Paul proclaimed to the Ephesians that they and he "have boldness" (Ephesians 3:12). He didn't say they should get it, but that they already had it. In the original Greek text *(parrésia)*, this word means confidence or boldness.[5] So what does this mean for us?

To have boldness and confidence means that you have the privilege to, at any time, approach the very throne of God. You never need to hide from the Almighty in fear. Boldness also allows you to dwell 24 hours a day in the presence of Christ. In fact, Jesus is personally present with you right now (Matthew 28:20). He is present in your heart, touches you through your thoughts and emotions, and makes His presence felt by the truth we read from His Word, by the love and mercy He gives us for others, by the strength He infuses in us.

Imagine: Jesus is just as close to you as He was to the people He met face to face while He was on earth. Jesus is *more near to us* than He was to the Pharisees and Sadducees when He talked to them. He is *at your side* just as He was with Matthew, Mark, Peter, and John. And He promises *to be with you* forever (Matthew 28:20).

Yes, we indeed have boldness. And we are practicing it daily as we go to the throne of God. We aren't timid, we aren't shy, we aren't hesitant to speak to Him. Now, is it possible to have this same boldness toward others? Can we be like the Shulammite woman, who said of her husband, "My beloved is mine, and I am His" (Song of Solomon 2:16)? Yes, we can, as we eliminate the hindrances of timidity, shyness, and whatever else might keep us from being bold. The key here is to develop determination.

Developing Boldness Through Determination

Have you noticed how young children who are Christians are frequently zealous about telling others about Christ? They don't seem the slightest bit hindered by what others may think. They simply focus on the fact that Jesus is in heaven, and how wonderful it would be if everyone else were there with Him someday.

Many years ago, when our family went shopping for a used car, my then-six-year-old son, Johnathan, showed that kind of innocent boldness when he reminded me of the need to share Christ with the car salesman. Taking me aside, he said with determination, "Mom, we can't leave this car lot until he accepts Jesus!"

Johnathan and I ended up sharing with this salesman until 11 PM! (we had arrived at the car lot before noon). Because the car lot was closing at that hour we were forced to leave, but we had further opportunities, by telephone, to continue that lengthy conversation about Jesus with that salesman. He was genuinely interested in what we shared, and he even began to have concerns for his wife's spiritual condition as well.

Does our passion to invest in the kingdom of heaven have this child-like determination? If not, how can we develop such determination? *By not being intimidated by others.* We briefly mentioned this earlier, but how can we make that real? By speaking with confidence. Back when Peter and John first started sharing the gospel after Jesus' ascension into heaven, the crowds in Jerusalem "observed the confidence of Peter and John and understood that they were uneducated and untrained men, [and] they were amazed, and began to recognize them as having been with Jesus" (Acts 4:13).

While Peter and John might have been uneducated, they knew they had God's truth. That was their source of confidence, a confidence that was founded in the fact they themselves had been with Jesus and seen and heard the truth firsthand. You, too, as a Christian, possess the truth. You know how God desires for people to live. You know that only Jesus Christ can redeem people for their lostness in sin. You know the eternal destiny of those who don't come to Christ. God's truth backs you up, and thus, you can have complete confidence.

By the way, have you ever considered that unbelievers are usually more willing to hear about Jesus than they will let on? I firmly believe that most unbelievers have at least some admiration for Jesus Christ in spite of their rejection of Him, and that can form some common ground between us and them.

You may be skeptical that some unbelievers have an admiration for Jesus. But consider: Even non-Christians quote from the Bible. You may have heard unbelievers quote from the Sermon on the Mount: "Blessed are the poor....blessed are those who mourn....blessed are the peace-makers..." (Matthew 5:3-4,9).

Jews, Muslims, and even some atheists admire Jesus. The atheist philosopher Friedrich Nietzsche (1844–1900), who became famous for saying, "God is dead!" also said there was "only one Christian and he died on the cross."[6] While on the surface unbelievers will reject Christ and mock Christianity, deep down inside they may actually admire Christ or wish they knew the same peace and joy you have as a Christian.

One key step in building determination is to be patient with non-Christians. *There will be people who get upset with you.* Why? Because in our conversation, it will eventually come up that Jesus died on a cross *for their sins.* Some people will flat out deny they could possibly be a sinner. "How dare you!" they may exclaim.

Others will get upset when we talk about giving up our life of sin, or crucifying the flesh. The Holy Spirit may convict them, making them realize that they, too, need to crucify "the flesh with its passions and desires" (Galatians 5:24). We need to keep in mind that "the word of the cross is foolishness to those who are perishing" (1 Corinthians 1:18). No matter how sensitive we try to be (and sensitivity is *very* important), the cross and the crucified life are an offense to the unbeliever, so you need to expect that some will get upset. But make sure you don't avoid sharing Christ out of fear that you might upset someone. You want to think of the bigger picture—the person's salvation.

Developing Boldness by Making It a Habit

You may be thinking, *There is no way I can be a bold person. That just isn't me!* You are mistaken. You *can* be bold because boldness isn't a matter of changing your personality. Rather, it's a matter of getting your mind off yourself and onto Christ. Timidity and shyness come from thinking too much about self and what others may think. Boldness thinks about Jesus and calls up the courage to share with others out of a concern for their eternal destiny.

Do you remember Joseph of Arimathea, a member of the Jewish Council (Mark 15:43) and Nicodemus, "a ruler of the Jews" (John 3:1)?

They were not bold; they were secret followers of Christ. It was said of Joseph of Arimathea that he was "a disciple of Jesus, but a secret one for fear of the Jews" (John 19:38). And, it appears that Nicodemus may have been a secret follower because he first sought Jesus by night (John 3:1; 7:50; 19:39).

Boldness can be a part of our lifestyle when we *form the habit* to be bold. How do habits get formed? By doing a specific action again and again to the point it becomes a natural part of you or your character. That's exactly what is done when we injure a muscle and receive physical rehabilitation. The injured muscle is slowly conditioned into being used again and again until it functions normally. Forming godly habits is a lot like getting a muscle back into shape—we must repeatedly exercise the behavior that we want to make into a habit.

The first step to cultivating the habit of boldness is *forgetting self*. Look at how Joseph of Arimathea and Nicodemus forgot about self. After the crucifixion, they stripped themselves of all timidity, and boldly pursued, in daylight,[7] the body of Jesus. This is quite remarkable. Now let's zoom in for a closer look at what took place. Joseph went directly to Pilate and asked permission for Jesus' body. (John 19:38). As soon as he got that permission, he ran to Golgotha and claimed the body. At this time it's still daylight, so any Jews who saw this may have asked, "Isn't this Joseph of Arimathea, one of the members of the Sanhedrin? What does he want with the body of Jesus?" And imagine the further surprise when they saw who came with Joseph to help carry the body away. It was Nicodemus (John 19:38-39),[8] their Jewish leader! Not only do the onlookers see these men claim the body, but they also realize their intent to follow the Jewish custom of preparing the body with spices and wrapping it in linen for burial (John 19:39-40). Consider how appalled the onlookers might have been—earlier, they had shouted "Crucify Him!" (John 19:15), and now they saw two of their leaders treating Jesus' body with respect and honor. It is reasonable to believe that from that moment on, Joseph of Arimathea and Nicodemus were ostracized from the Jewish community. They may have lost their high positions and the respect and honor that had been given to them. By their actions, they showed everyone that they were no longer secret and timid followers of Jesus, but bold believers. And it happened because their priorities had become Christ-centered. Are the things of Christ truly a priority in your life?

Next, *think about what would help others spiritually.* What is best for them in any given situation? Look at the apostle Paul. Although he was called to preach to the Gentiles, he made a habit ("custom," Acts 17:2) of first preaching to the Jews in whatever town he went into (Acts 17:2,10,17; 9:20). Paul first went to the Jews because he knew they wouldn't listen to him if he had gone to the Gentiles first, whereas the Gentiles would not have minded his going to the Jews first. So Paul followed a strategy based on knowing his audience.

We too can be strategic, and that brings us to our next point: *praying for the lost.* Paul said, "My heart's desire and my prayer to God for them is for their salvation" (Romans 10:1). Who do you know that needs to consider Jesus? How might you pray for them daily? Perhaps at each meal? Perhaps during your family Bible study?

Next, we can increase our habit of boldness *by learning what others believe* so that we can adequately share with them (2 Timothy 2:15). We don't need to feel intimidated by this. Demonstrating His love and passion for the lost, Jesus said in a parable, "Rejoice with me, for I have found my sheep which was lost!" (Luke 15:6). At that moment, Jesus wasn't thinking about the masses. He was focusing on just that one sheep. Jesus said, "I tell you that in the same way, there will be more joy in heaven over one sinner who repents, than over ninety-nine righteous persons who need no repentance" (Luke 15:7).

God hasn't called each of us to reach the whole world. All we need this very moment is to reach out to that one, or perhaps few, whom God has brought into our sphere of influence. Focusing upon that one—perhaps your neighbor, friend, or co-worker—you can first inquire about what she believes. Is she a Jehovah's Witness or a Mormon? Is she Jewish or a Catholic? Is she into the New Age movement? Whatever she believes, begin reaching out to her by going to the local Christian bookstore and buying a book about her beliefs. The book will not only help you understand what she believes, but also will help you understand what God's Word says about those beliefs and how they contradict Scripture. After learning and getting equipped, slowly but surely, start talking to your neighbor, friend, or co-worker about particular topics in her belief system. Use God's Word to draw her to the life-saving truth (again, the book you purchase will help you). What joy there is in giving that one person the inspired, God-breathed Word (2 Timothy 3:16)! It *will* make a difference in that person's life (Isaiah 55:11).

We can also strengthen our habit of boldness by *showing hospitality to the lost.* In a world where people no longer open their homes to others, do you know what a blessing it would be for you to invite an unbelieving friend or acquaintance to your home for dinner? People are thirsty for someone to show friendship, care, and interest in them. In due time, people won't be able to help but see that you belong to Jesus and He belongs to you. Other possibilities include giving food to the needy, befriending an aloof neighbor, starting an evangelistic Bible study in a retirement home or your neighborhood. If you are a college student, you could reach out to a student who is eating lunch alone.

Finally, it's vital that as we cultivate the habit of boldness, we do so with *sensitivity and care for the lost.* Insensitivity is all around us. In this world, we see coldness toward the unborn, the physically challenged, the "different," and the elderly. I've seen insensitivity in the church, too. I've seen believers speak to nonbelievers in such a condescending way I just want to cringe. I've also been saddened to see Christians who don't want to have anything to do with nonbelievers.

I'll never forget a conversation I had with a group of young women, all raised in Christian homes. As they talked, they said they didn't have any non-believing friends, they didn't like nonbelievers, and they thought that most of them were "strange." Each one then shared negative stories about non-Christians who lived in their neighborhoods. I asked the women, "Don't you have any desire to reach them for Christ?" They looked at me in unison as if I were nuts and exclaimed, "No!"

I then said, "Had you said that decades ago, then you would be saying that you had no desire to reach out to me. Had you made your remark four centuries ago, you would have been saying you didn't want to reach out to

> *W*hen people see you care for them, they will trust you when you talk to them about the Lord.

people like John Bunyan [the famous writer of the allegorical story *The Pilgrim's Progress*]. Had you made your remarks 2,000 years ago, you would have been saying you didn't want to reach out to the apostles or to women such as Mary Magdalene, Dorcas, Priscilla, and Phoebe."

While we who are Christians know it's wrong to live in sin, we have to realize that nonbelievers are unable to live righteously because they don't have Jesus. They can't live pure lives, and their language may at times be foul. We have to expect we won't be comfortable at times around non-Christians.

We need to push aside the externals and think about the heart. Realize that non-Christians want love and care just as much as we do. They have needs, and because we know God's truth and possess His love in us, we are equipped to care for these souls and bring them to Christ—rather than just leave them alone.

As women of spiritual passion, we should say, "If others do not care, I will see to it that I care." We ought to live as Jesus lived. He cared tremendously. He felt great compassion for the widow of Nain (Luke 7:13-15), for the blind and the lame (Matthew 21:14), the lepers (Mark 1:40-42), and the paralyzed (Luke 5:17-26). He expressed great concern for the people of Jerusalem (Matthew 23:37-39). Jesus lived out the old saying, "People don't care how much you know until you show them how much you care." When people see you care for them, they will trust you when you talk to them about the Lord.

Now, in our endeavor to be bold, we must make sure we don't cross the line into tactlessness. What some people call boldness is really a lack of tact, and we need to know there's a difference between the two.

Developing a Boldness That Is Tactful

I experienced firsthand the tactlessness of others when I was a 21-year-old nonbeliever. I had just visited a Christian church *for the very first time.* It was very difficult for me to even step foot in that church because having been raised as a Catholic, I had been taught it would be a mortal sin to do so. Thankfully, the Spirit of God was working in me, and I did attend that church service.

After the service, three guys—students from the local Christian college—found out from the person who invited me that I was *not* a Christian. So right after the service they approached me, introduced themselves, and without any other informal chit-chat, they blurted out, "We just want you to know *you are not a Christian;* therefore, you are on your way to hell."

Let me ask the obvious: What non-Christian would be anxious to hear more of what we have to say about God after an introduction like that? Sadly, the introduction I received from those three men is not uncommon. A while ago a Christian woman boasted to me, saying, "I met a stranger today on the bus, and the first thing I said to him was, 'You're going to hell!'"

Wanting to cringe, I asked, "What was his response?"

She replied, "He looked away from me, but at least he knows he's going to hell."

Now, it's true every lost soul must be aware of his or her true spiritual condition and where he or she is going for eternity. I certainly needed to consider my spiritual state when told I was on my way to hell. But being blunt and tactless toward an unbeliever isn't the way to help.

Church father Augustine (A.D. 354–430) quoted orator, lawyer, politician, and philosopher Marcus Tullius Cicero (106–43 B.C.) as saying that in trying to persuade others toward truth, we should not neglect three things—that is, we are "to teach, to delight, and to move."[9] Augustine expanded upon Cicero's comment, saying that,

> To teach is a necessity, to delight is a beauty, to persuade is a triumph. Now of these three, the one first mentioned, the teaching, which is a matter of necessity, depends on what we say; the other two *on the way we say it.*[9]

It's so important to communicate truth in a loving way, for it's then that we get the attention of the listener. Look at Jesus. He not only taught the people and delighted them, but also lovingly persuaded them. He was able to do these three things because of the kindness He showed to unbelievers, such as the Samaritan woman (John 4:1-42). He confronted her sin but did so in a sensitive way (John 4:16-18), without condemning her and telling her she was on her way to hell. Rather, He made sure He offered her a solution, telling her she needed to worship God "in spirit and in truth" (John 4:24).

And remember how He treated lovingly the woman caught in adultery? Then there was Zaccheus, the tax collector. Jesus didn't point a finger at him and declare he was a thief. No, He reached out to this man in a personable and friendly way, meeting him where he was. Through Jesus' love and acceptance of these people, they came to their own conclusions regarding their sin. Jesus was in the business of giving the "living water" of divine truth and inviting people toward that water.

We can learn from Jesus and apply His example as we reach out to others. And when we do, we will reap the reward of their being persuaded.

Recently, I saw such a transformation through persuasion while sharing Christ with an atheist as we sat together on a bus for two hours. I was coming home from a television tour, and she was coming back to the States after visiting her homeland the Czech Republic. During the first half hour or so, Vlasta told me why she had moved to the United States some ten years ago. She then asked why I was on the bus. I told her about my TV interviews for one of my books, which naturally led to the discussion of my faith in Jesus and what He came to do for mankind. Vlasta admitted she knew very little about Jesus. You should have seen her face when she heard me quote, "For God so loved the world, that He sent His only begotten Son, that whoever believes in Him shall not perish, but have eternal life" (John 3:16). As I explained this verse to Vlasta, she began nodding her head and said with firm conviction, "There is hope in this world." No words can describe what I was feeling when she made that statement.

Vlasta is now reading the Bible for the first time and wants to learn all she can about Jesus. Imagine how she might have responded if I had tactlessly told her that she was going to hell because she was an atheist. She would have had no understanding of Christian love, nor would she have come to realize there was any hope for her. She now knows there is. Again, it all goes back to not only teaching truth, but the way we communicate it.

Perhaps today there are loving words
Which Jesus would have me speak,
There may be now,
in the paths of sin,
Some wand'rer whom I should seek;
O Savior, if Thou wilt be my Guide

Tho dark and rugged the way,
My voice shall echo the message sweet
I'll say what You want me to say.[10]

Attracting Others to Christ

Brian and I have a friend named Mike. About five years ago, Mike asked me, "Why is it that you born-againers are so persistent about trying to convince people like me? Why can't you leave us alone?"

I replied, "Because we want you to have what we have—a wonderful relationship with Jesus Christ, and assurance of salvation. Life is so wonderful because of Jesus."

Mike dismissed the fact that Jesus was the answer and often called us fanatics. But recently, Mike became a Christian. Yes, he became one of us born-againers, one of those people who won't "leave others alone."

After Mike became a Christian, he said to me, "Donna, I was mad at you, deep inside my soul, *for years!* And it wasn't because of what you shared, but what I saw. I was absolutely jealous of you."

"What did you see that made you so jealous?" I asked.

Mike answered, "I saw joy and peace in you, regardless of what you were going through in life. You were always so happy. I really wanted what you have—that blissful relationship with Jesus. But my pride couldn't admit how miserable I really was, and that I too needed Christ."

People like Mike can't help but be attracted to the special relationship that we have with Jesus. *All that He is…*is ours! His righteousness, acceptableness, worthiness, wisdom, strength, resurrection, life. And *all that we had…*became His! Our sin, guilt, sorrow, and shame were all taken up by Him onto Himself and away from us *forever!*

How could others *not* be attracted to the One we lean upon, we dwell with, we bear all our burdens to? How could they *not* be impressed with the One who provides for all our needs, who conquers all our foes, and who delivers us from hell and prepares a place for us in heaven?

The Bridegroom has given us, His bride, *everything* (2 Peter 1:3). And among the things He has given us is a field—"the field is the world" (Matthew 13:38). And it's this field Jesus was speaking of when He said, "Go into all the world and preach the gospel to all creation" (Mark 16:15). Telling others about our relationship with Jesus is not an option. As we can see, it's a command. I can understand such a command—back when I married Brian, I wanted *all women* to know that he was now married. He, of course, wanted *all men* to know that I too was married.

True love doesn't hide one's beloved. It boldly proclaims, "I belong to that person." Have we become content with limiting our talk about Jesus to Sundays? As women of spiritual passion, women who love our Bridegroom, we ought to make Him known in all circles of our lives. We ought to have no friend whom we cannot introduce to Jesus. We ought to take great joy in letting others see that *Jesus is mine, and I am His.*

Our Passion in Action

1. What hindrances keep you from sharing Christ with others? What can you do to lovingly reach out to others?

2. Think for an entire day about the reality of hell. Imagine what it would be like to be sent to that place of destruction. How does this affect your perspective of your unsaved family members, friends, and acquaintances? Praise God for sparing you, but also, think of those you know who are on their way there.

3. Begin a prayer journal that lists the names those who need Jesus. Write prayers for their specific needs, if you know them. Also, save some room for answered prayer! Make a concerted effort to pray for these people daily.

4. Decide this week one person you will start reaching out to in a practical way. Take some active steps toward graciously pursuing this individual. Will it be a lunch or dinner invitation? A phone call to inquire how she is doing? A letter to let her know you've been thinking about her?

5. What other habits not mentioned in this chapter can you form as you cultivate the determination to reach others for Christ?

11

Enduring in Total Devotion

"I will rejoice greatly in the LORD, my soul will exult in my God."
—ISAIAH 61:10

Twenty-five years ago (although it seems like just yesterday!) I enrolled in a Monday-through-Friday jogging class at college. My reason was simple. I wanted jogging to become a permanent part of my lifestyle.

On the first day of class, there were about 15 of us spread out on the grass of the athletic field. The instructor, whom we'll call "Coach Runner," seemed more like a drill sergeant than an athletic coach as he went over, point by point, the expectations he had of us. As I listened to what I thought were *impossible* expectations, I began to think, *I'm in the wrong class!* My thoughts were interrupted by Coach Runner, who was shouting, "I'm going to train you hard—so hard—you'll be begging for mercy!"

Coach Runner then told us that from our class, he was going to select the "cream of the crop" for a jogging team he was forming. This team would compete with other schools. At the time I didn't know other colleges had jogging teams, and I still don't know if they do. But Coach Runner was passionate about forming this "team."

Then Coach Runner asked, "Any questions?"

I raised my hand, and Coach Runner said gruffly, "Permission to speak."

I said quite casually, "Coach Runner, I am *obviously* in the wrong class. I just wanted to take a nice little class, nothing serious, just something to help me get into the lifestyle of jogging. May I leave now?"

Coach Runner asked, "What is your name?"

Thinking he was going to cross me off his attendance sheet, I stood up, dusted myself off, and with a sense of relief said, "Donna." Before I could give him my last name, he said, "Ah! Here you are."

The coach circled my name on his chart and then looked at me with stern eyes. "No one, I mean no one, quits my classes. Not even you. If you say you want to become a jogger, I expect to see you tomorrow morning, 8:00 AM sharp!"

I sat back down, silenced. I didn't know what to say. But I must admit, Coach Runner motivated me with that one word, "If…." Yes, I did want to be a jogger, and Coach Runner made me feel that I could possibly become one. So despite the unconventional ways of the coach, I showed up the next morning.

Coach Runner pushed us hard. Each day before we started to "learn" how to run, we had to do many warm-up exercises. And after we ran, we did cool-down exercises. The warm-up stretching was to prepare our bodies for the run, and the same stretching afterwards was to help cool down our bodies. Doing all those exercises painfully woke up my muscles! I thought to myself, *Coach, why not just shoot me now and get it over with?*

The coach had us do the "hurdler's exercise" (which looks like Rodan's "The Thinker" doing his warm-ups), the "fencer" (ready for a duel, anyone?), the "fish" (this exercise looks quite strange to the unknowing eye), the thigh stretch (ouch!), and on and on it went. There was the side stretch, the standing spinal twist, the plough, the shoulder stand, the leg lifts, the one-leg stretch, and the twisted-side bend. As if that weren't enough, we also had to do the forward bends, the neck roll, the toe touch, the side bend, and lest I forget, the sit-ups and those unforgettable push-ups—ugh!

After all that, Coach Runner would blow his whistle and say, "Alright, enough relaxation. Let's get running!"

One day I learned from Coach Runner a lesson that has stayed with me all these years. I had already been jogging for about a mile when I suddenly felt a sharp pain in my side and bent over. The coach came running out to the field. I thought he was coming out to show me a little compassion. *How nice,* I thought. Well, I was wrong. With his face turning a deep red, Coach Runner hollered, "Don't stop! Get running! Get running!"

I cried out, "I'm getting cramps—I can't!"

Coach Runner said, "Don't say you can't. Yes, you can! If you want to take jogging seriously you must realize that pain—pain that doesn't inhibit movement—is normal. You've got to expect it; you've got to deal with it. Take the pain with you as you run. Work with it. Now, get running!"[1]

And so I did. I ran each morning and took the pain with me. By the end of the class, I was jogging six miles a day. In case you're wondering, no, I didn't get chosen for the coach's jogging team. That's okay, because that wasn't my goal. I just wanted to know how to jog, and I got more than I bargained for.

When I became a Christian one year later, I found it fascinating that the apostle Paul uses the metaphor of running a race to describe the Christian life (1 Corinthians 9:24-27 and more).[2] What might have inspired him to write about Christians running as if in a race?

Paul's Inspiration

During the days of Paul, athletic games of all sorts were popular. There were the Olympic games in Greece, the Pythian games at Delphi, the Isthmian games at Corinth, the Nemean games at Argos, and the Panatheneaea at Athens.[3]

Track events meant everything to the runners because they had to work so hard to even be selected for the race. Only the very best were chosen from the local and municipal elimination trials. After ten months of rigorous training under professional gymnasts, the runners were examined by officials. If still in good shape, they were selected and then were to take an oath to obey all competition rules. And finally, these races meant a lot to the runners because they wanted to win the prize, a laurel wreath—a very prestigious award, as we'll see in a moment.

When Paul wanted to illustrate the discipline of the Christian life, he used the example of running, which required intense athletic training. Paul also wants the spiritual race to mean everything to us, because "only one receives the prize" (1 Corinthians 9:24), an "imperishable" wreath (1 Corinthians 9:25). Just for the record, winning the prize has nothing to do with obtaining salvation.[4]

Paul's Exhortation

Like a herald at the ancient athletic games, who proclaimed the rules and the conditions of the contest and summoned the runners to the starting line, so Paul is exhorting us in this spiritual race. He encourages us to run this race well: "Run in such a way that you may win" (1 Corinthians 9:4).

Running to Win

We have to wonder: Why would a runner go through such rigorous training simply to win a laurel wreath? Because while the wreath was the only prize given at the athletic games, there were far greater rewards ahead. Many athletes, upon returning home from their triumph, would be rewarded with great sums of money. Some cities offered their athletes government positions. Musicians would sing their praise, poets and writers would record their skill and courage, and the crowds would idolize their hero—so openly, that jealous philosophers complained. Because of the wonderful future that awaited a winner, the athletes were most definitely preoccupied with winning.

You may be thinking, *Why must I win? Can't I just run? If "only one receives the prize," wouldn't it be more loving to allow a brother or sister in Christ to win instead of me? I'm content with being in second place.*

On the surface such an attitude may seem admirable. But may I be so bold as to encourage you that *you* need to run so as to win? There is nothing selfish, covetous, or sinful in this because your pursuit is spiritual. Earthly striving does thrust people aside, but we're talking now about becoming women of spiritual passion. We are above all that. We know that our striving in this race isn't earthly, it's heavenly. It isn't secular, it's spiritual. Being this is a heavenly race, all we are casting aside is secular ambition. And as we pursue the imperishable wreath, which is also called the "crown of righteousness" (2 Timothy 4:8), the "crown of life" (James 1:12; Revelation 2:10), and the "unfading crown of glory" (1 Peter 5:4), we will spur onward our passion for spiritual things. What's more, our zeal may help motivate other believers, inspiring them to pursue the same passion. As we run the race with excellence, we will also become a blessing to all those around us. How could we not when we're pursuing the crown of righteousness? See how important it is to run so as to win that incorruptible crown, as if we are the only ones who could wear it? And we do this not for ourselves, but for God. By our striving, we are pleasing Jesus—we are doing what His Word tells us to do—win (1 Corinthians 9:24).

> *A*t conversion we are invited to take our part on the racecourse and join the heavenly race.

Starting the Race

At conversion we are invited to take our part on the racecourse and join the heavenly race (1 Corinthians 9:24-25). The starting line is at the foot of the cross, and the finish line is in heaven. The race is short for some, longer for others, but regardless of length, we are all called to run with intensity. This run demands all of our energy. And to be a successful runner, we must lay "aside every encumbrance" (Hebrews 12:1). That's exactly what we've been challenged to do throughout this book—to set aside the hindrances that diminish our spiritual passion. These hindrances include our hurts, fears, anxiety about our needs, wrong views of God's love, spiritual lukewarmness, weak faith, the presence of sin in our hearts, living beneath our circumstances, an inadequate approach to feeding upon God's Word, and a fear of sharing God with others. We know by now that part of being spiritually passionate is being ever active and aggressive at overcoming our hindrances. We cannot be satisfied with anything short of dealing with them so that we may win the race and become the women we desire to be.

Now that we've talked about these obstacles and how to overcome them, let's learn how we can excel in running the race with the full knowledge that without the grace of God, we would not be able to run at all (Philippians 2:13).

Winning the Race

Step 1: Preparation Through Exercise

Remember all the stretching exercises Coach Runner had the class do before jogging? They, of course, were for a purpose—to keep our muscles flexible and strong, to help us run much better. Without stretching, we simply wouldn't have been able to jog as well as we would like. Paul surely understood the importance of warm-up exercises in the athletic games, and even more so in the spiritual race.

One of the ways we can "exercise" is by *training our imperfect heart, mind, and soul toward greater spiritual growth*. We can strain and reach passionately, using our energy to search the Scriptures, think deeply about what we read, meditate upon key verses, and pray for guidance from the Holy Spirit. These are what move us forward to win the race. Second Timothy 3:16 says that "all Scripture is inspired by God and profitable for teaching, for reproof, for correction, for *training in righteousness;* so that the man of God may be adequate, equipped for every good work."

Another part of our training, a very important part, is to exercise *self-control.* Paul said that "everyone who competes in the games exercises self-control *in all things*" (1 Corinthians 9:25). Paul knew that if an athlete didn't resist indulgence, if he didn't work at firming his muscles or building up his body to full strength, he wouldn't be able to bear the fatigue and strain of athletic competition.

Through self-control we too must resist indulgence and work at eliminating anything that could slow us down and cause us fatigue as we run. Let's discern. Does our tongue slow us down (1 Timothy 5:13)? What about wrongful attitudes (Philippians 2:14), wrongful thoughts (Psalm 139:23-24), or anger (James 1:19-20)? What about personal purity (1 Thessalonians 4:3-5)? If we're not careful, the flesh could end up controlling us, rather than we controlling it. That's where the exercise comes in—*with the asking of the Holy Spirit for help,* since our "spirit is willing, but the flesh is weak" (Mark 14:38).

Step 2: Don't Look Back

Every trained runner knows the number-one rule in a race: *Don't look back!* This slows them down, and when it comes to running, literally every hundredth of a second counts. One look back can cost a runner the race.

Paul tells us not to look back by "forgetting what lies behind" (Philippians 3:13). This is for our own good. Dwelling on the past keeps us down, keeps us ineffective, keeps us from winning the race. Paul spoke from experience. Consider how difficult it might have been for him to forget his past. He had been responsible for the imprisonment and deaths of Christians (Acts 8:1-3 and more[5]). He could have let his awful past eat him up alive. But he wouldn't allow it. As well, he could have become bitter over the cruel things others had done to him (2 Corinthians 11:23-26). He wouldn't allow that either. He could have looked back to more prosperous days, but instead he said, "I have learned to be content in whatever circumstances I am" (Philippians 4:11). Paul knew that to be successful in running the race, he had to forget all the past and reach forward "to what lies ahead" (Philippians 3:13).

You may be thinking, *Easier said than done!* I agree. Yet we *can* forget our past—our sins, our failures, our regrets—when we leave it all at the cross. Because of the atoning power of Jesus we are freed from *everything* in our past. There's no need for us to worry about the very things Christ has already taken care of for us.

As we leave our past at the nail-scarred feet of Jesus, we free ourselves to run at full strength, to run without becoming weary (Isaiah 40:31) as our "inner man is being renewed day by day" (2 Corinthians 4:16).

Step 3: Concentrate

Paul reinforces our need to concentrate on the effort at hand when he says, "One thing I do" (Philippians 3:13). To concentrate is to focus on one objective without any halfheartedness. Paul says that this "one thing" is striving toward perfection in our spiritual life (Philippians 3:12). Obviously, we will never know perfection on this side of heaven, but our desire should be for our lives to be as wholly consecrated as possible for our Lord.

What aspect of your spiritual life do you think you need to concentrate on so you can run more effectively? Is it purity? A more consistent prayer life? Spending more time with Jesus? Whatever your spiritual need is at this moment—concentrate, focus, stay put by enriching this area in your life. When you grow in that area, focus on the next you may feel you need to grow in. Again, while we'll never reach perfection in this lifetime, we shouldn't stop striving. Running is all about reaching goals. Let us never allow anything to stop us from our goals, not even if we are in pain. Instead, let's run in spite of the pain.

Step 4: Run with the Pain

Remember when Coach Runner told me to keep running even

while I was in pain? At the time, I felt his command was insensitive. But now I understand it. Had I stopped, I would never have pushed my limit of endurance. I would not have developed greater stamina. I would have been training myself to stop anytime I even felt a tinge of pain.

Maybe you are experiencing pain right now. Such pain is unavoidable; we're to expect it. Don't let it stop you from running.

Enduring the Pain

Paul had the right perspective when it comes to pain. He said that our "momentary, light affliction is producing for us an eternal weight of glory far beyond all comparison" (2 Corinthians 4:17). You may be asking, "Are you calling my afflictions *light?*" No, I'm not, but Paul is. When we're in the midst of our pain, we will wonder, *How could he call any affliction "light"?* After all, how light is the pain

> *Whatever our affliction, it is momentary compared to eternity.*

from the death of a loved one, or an incurable illness? Sometimes our pain can bring on such deep, intense sorrow that we don't want to keep running the race. Instead, we want to crawl into a hole and die, like Job (Job 3:3,11,25-26). It's certainly a fact that in this life, we won't always be roaming through green pastures or sitting beside still waters. Life is often bleak, rugged, and mountainous. It is marked by trails of trouble, strain, and sorrow. So then, why does Paul call our afflictions *light?* Because they are *momentary* (2 Corinthians 4:17). In other words, our pain will not last. It will come to an end. Take a look at Paul. We already know that his afflictions were many, and that they had to be emotionally draining, but they were only *for a moment.* Look at Jesus on the cross. No one can say His horrible, excruciating six hours of torture, along with the agony of carrying the sins of the world, was light. But even that suffering was but *for a moment.*

Truly, momentary pain, like that experienced by a woman giving birth to a child, will be forgotten. Therefore we must look at the greater thing, which is eternity. Whatever our affliction, it is momentary compared to eternity, and it is light compared with the eternal "weight of glory" spoken of in 2 Corinthians 4:17. So even though pain is real, Paul tells us to keep running, to "run with endurance" (Hebrews 12:1). And by keeping our eye on the prize—an eternity with God in heaven—we can indeed run the race to the finish line.

Running with Endurance

As we learned in chapter 6, endurance is so important in our spiritual life. We discovered that as we "let endurance have its perfect result" we can be "perfect and complete, lacking in nothing" (James 1:4). Jesus Himself knew the importance of endurance and told us to persevere to the end (Matthew 10:22). In other words, "Don't stop!" just as Coach Runner told me. Endurance is what gives us the power to withstand pain, hardship, and stress.

In addition, endurance allows our devotion for Jesus to grow. Open up to just about any book in the Bible, and you will see endurance at work in the lives of God's people. Whether their soul was filled with great joy or burdened with sorrow, whether they were rejoicing over a victory won or burdened by fear, whether the presence of God was enjoyed or whether His face seemed hidden, amid all changes and feelings and situations—from the blackest thundercloud to the brightest of sunshine—these people endured. How could they? Because of their loyalty to God. They would risk their very lives for Him, without the asking, all because their eyes were fixed upon the Almighty as they patiently endured to the end. As we run the race, we too can develop enduring devotion by "fixing our eyes on Jesus" (Hebrews 12:2), not taking our eyes off Him for a moment.

Fixing Our Eyes on Jesus

Being "fixed" on Jesus is what enables us to patiently endure, to bear suffering well, to absorb all pain and loss for Him. He is worthy of all that we have, for better or for worse, for richer or for poorer, in sickness and in health. We as His bride will endure until the end, laying whatever we can at His feet, gracefully accepting all that comes our way in this spiritual race. Truly, Jesus looks upon us with pleasure when He sees a reflection of Himself as we enter into His own sufferings. We become partakers with Him of the cup of His sufferings (Matthew 20:22)—a cup that not every believer is eager to drink.

Have you ever noticed, in an athletic race, that some of the fastest runners at the beginning of the race run out of energy partway through and end up slowing down before they reach the finish line? That happens because of a lack of endurance. We don't want to slow down in the spiritual race—and to prevent that from happening, we need to keep our focus fixed on Jesus.

Those who are not completely focused and committed in life are "double minded" and "unstable" in all their ways, according to James 1:8. But those who maintain their focus have what they need to run the race successfully. This includes the fruit of the Spirit, such as patience (Galatians 5:22), the "encouragement of the Scriptures" (Romans 15:4), and God-given perseverance (Romans 15:5). We also have the assurance of God's love and care, and His promise to rescue us when we need help (Psalm 119:153). And we can be assured that we will always have grace according to our need (Hebrews 4:16).

Therefore, "do not lose heart" (2 Corinthians 4:16). If we lose heart, we lose strength. So here's the challenge. If secular athletes will give all their energy, all their pain, and all their hope toward winning a corruptible prize, how much more enthusiasm and effort should those of us who are spiritual athletes give toward winning an incorruptible crown? A garland of leaves and a day's popularity cannot even compare with our reward: Jesus and eternity.

Our Inspiration

Imagine that you are running your final steps in the spiritual race. Up ahead, at the finish line, you see your Bridegroom's arms stretched out to receive you. As He takes hold of you, you hear the happy shouts and encouragements of a great cloud of witnesses (Hebrews 12:1) who had gone before you—the Old Testament prophets who were rejected, the New Testament apostles who walked the arduous and dusty roads with Christ, the martyrs of the ages who shed their blood in the name of Jesus, the countless sufferers who rejoiced in their tribulation; the myriad of children who entered early into the arms of Jesus; and all other ages, ranks, and testimonies of men and women who have already finished the race and are cheering you on. And the wreath that you receive—the crown of righteousness (2 Timothy 4:8)—you will immediately place at Jesus' feet, knowing that it was His grace and power that made the crown possible. Because that crown was won for Him, it will be worn by Him. And for the rest of eternity, when you see that crown, you will remember the blood, sweat, and tears shed for that crown—a crown that reveals the spiritual passion you had for Jesus while on earth. And like Paul you will be able to say, "I have fought the good fight, I have finished the course, I have kept the faith" (2 Timothy 4:7).

Your wedding gift to Jesus will be your crown. And what will His gift to you be, along with eternal life? Here's a hint:

> It was given to her to clothe herself in fine linen,
> bright and clean;
> for the fine linen is the righteous acts of the saints.[6]
> Enter into the joy of the Master.[7]

Our Passion in Action

1. Read 1 Corinthians 9:24. Why should you run to win? Why won't second place do?

2. What action can you take to warm up and stretch your spiritual muscles?

3. What areas of your life need more self-control? What will you do, starting today, to implement that?

4. How might you view your current affliction as "light"? Why would this help you find it easier to run the race?

5. In what new ways might you show outwardly your devotion to Jesus?

6. When you get to the finish line, what are the first words you would like to say to Jesus? What would you like Him to tell you?

Appendix:
Do You Belong to Jesus?

I once had the opportunity to talk about spiritual matters to a woman named Marguerite. She said to me, "I've been a Christian all my life. My grandparents were Christians, my parents are Christians, and so am I. Since I can remember, I've been told that 'I am a Christian.'"

I asked Marguerite, "Can you define for me what a Christian is?"

Caught off guard, Marguerite said, "Well, I guess you could say that a Christian is a good person."

I replied, "I know some atheists who are what you would define as 'good people.' So obviously, then, being a good person isn't the definition of being a 'Christian'—otherwise we would have to say that some atheists are Christians, too. I don't think those atheists would appreciate that!"

Possibly like Marguerite, you have grown up thinking you are a Christian because you try to be a good person. Or, perhaps you think you are a Christian because you are a regular churchgoer, or because your parents' or grandparents' prayers for you protected you into womanhood. Yet none of these things make you or me a Christian, nor do they show that we belong to Jesus.

Maybe your situation is different—perhaps you have never gone to church or had the benefit of another person's prayers on your behalf. But you have been interested in spiritual things, and have wanted to hear about Jesus. Yet for some reason, you have never chosen to explore further. And yet another possibility is that at one time you came very close to embracing Jesus and felt the emotional charge that comes from being called to make a commitment to Jesus, but you let the emotion pass and delayed making a decision.

Sometimes Jesus waits for years for us to become committed to Him and be affected by His love. He may have watched you since childhood, through your teen years, and adulthood. There are even elderly women who tremble towards life's close and put off making a commitment to Jesus. Sadly, they seem unable to make the effort even as they approach the threat of death.

Earlier, we saw Marguerite define a Christian as a good person. But we need to understand that salvation *is not* based upon being a good person or good works, but rather, upon marvelous, undeserving grace towards us. Here's what Ephesians 2:8-9 says:

> For by grace you have been saved through faith;
> and that not of yourselves,
> it is the gift of God;
> not as a result of works, so that no one may boast.

Salvation comes through Jesus Christ only. Jesus says, "I am the way, and the truth, and the life; no one comes to the Father but through Me" (John 14:6). This really makes sense, for why would Jesus die on the cross for our sins if we could get to heaven by being good? Paul the apostle says that if this were the case, "then Christ died needlessly" (Galatians 2:21).

Before any of us come to Jesus, we are spiritually dead and cannot see the beauty of the vibrant spiritual life that Christians have, which includes divine forgiveness, deliverance, assurance, love, and the evidence of divine action. Our eyes become opened to spiritual things when we belong to Jesus.

Belonging to Jesus

We belong to Jesus when we *repent*. Repentance is not what mankind would suggest, but it is what Jesus commands. He tells us to "repent" (Mark 1:15) because He knows the human heart, and according to His

Word, "all have sinned and fall short of the glory of God" (Romans 3:23). He knows that our own goodness, or righteousness, or "good works"— whatever we want to call it—is as "a filthy garment" (Isaiah 64:6).

Repentance is more than feeling badly about how we've fallen short. It is being willing to change our attitude toward wrongdoing. It entails a willingness to change our life's direction. For good reason, then, we need to come before God in humility and acknowledge our wrongdoing, and repent.

We belong to Jesus when we *believe and trust.* In other words, we don't just believe the facts (as important as they are), but we also trust God Himself for what He says about those facts. For instance, Jesus tells us to "believe in the gospel" (Mark 1:15). And what is the gospel? "Gospel" means "good news." Jesus is telling us to believe in the good news. What is the good news? The truth that you can completely be forgiven of all wrongdoing—as a free love gift from God! And it's more than having your slate wiped clean, it is *gaining the righteousness of Christ—God's own perfection:* "He made Him who knew no sin to be sin on our behalf, so that we might become the righteousness of God in Him" (2 Corinthians 5:21).

Isn't that good news? Isn't it worth believing? Isn't worth trusting God for? It most certainly is, and it's all for the taking because our Creator loves us so much. Oh, "what shall I render to the LORD for all His benefits toward me? I shall lift up the cup of salvation" (Psalm 116:12-13).

So how did God do all this? He sent Christ as a sacrifice for sin. In Christ, the God-man Jesus (John 1:1; 20:28) accepted the punishment for sin, which is death, by dying on the cross in our place. God's justice and love are thus both perfectly fulfilled. God raised Jesus from the dead (Romans 10:9), so He is not only our Savior, but also our Lord! (John 20:28, see endnote 1 for other claims of deity on page 239).

Would you like to belong to Jesus and receive God's complete forgiveness of your sins? Would you like to have a personal relationship with Him (Revelation 3:20)? Would you like to know, in your heart, the presence of the One who promises He will never leave you nor forsake you (Hebrews 13:5)? Then, *repent* of your sins, *trust* in the Lord Jesus Christ, and *confess* Him as Lord (Romans 10:1-10,13). When you do, you will belong to Jesus, now and forever. The Bible says, "if we *confess our sins*, He is faithful and righteous to forgive us our sins and to *cleanse* us from *all* unrighteousness" (1 John 1:9).

In case you are unsure about the guarantee of heaven, read the following promise:

> The testimony is this, that God has given us eternal life, and this life is in His Son. He who has the Son has the life; he who does not have the Son of God does not have the life. These things I have written to you who believe in the name of the Son of God, so that you may know that you have eternal life (1 John 5:11-13).

This certainly is good news, isn't it? Do you want to know with certainty that you have eternal life? Below is a sample prayer you may want to pray:

> Dear Father in heaven,
>
> I know I am a sinner and unable to save myself. I do believe that You love me, and that because of Your great mercy You sent Your Son, Jesus, to die on the cross for my sins. I believe Your Son's words when He says that He is the only way to You and heaven. And, so, through Jesus, I come to You asking You to forgive me of my every sin, and to bestow upon me Your free gift of eternal life. Thank You for giving me Jesus as my Lord, my Savior, and my Master. I earnestly desire to follow Him, learn of Him, and to show my love to Him by obeying His Word. Thank You for hearing my prayer and answering it, and for giving

> me new life here on earth and everlasting life with You
> in Heaven—my true home. Amen.

If you have made a decision for Christ, then, on the authority of God's Word, your sins are forgiven (Colossians 1:14), and they shall never be taken into account (Romans 4:7-8). You are now a child of God (John 1:12; Romans 8:16) and have become an heir to all of God's blessings (Romans 8:16-17). You are a new creature in Christ; "the old things passed away; behold, new things have come" (2 Corinthians 5:17). You are now "born again" (John 3:3), with God's Holy Spirit living in you to guide and direct you (John 14:16-17). You now possess everlasting life (1 John 5:12-13) and belong to Jesus, now and *forever!* (John 14:2-3).

Now That You Belong to Jesus

One of the marvelous benefits of belonging to Jesus is that we have been given hope. Hope is the confident expectation of something quite wonderful. Far from disaster, tragedy, or pain, we hope for the opposite—pleasure, happiness, peace, and love. The foundation of our hope is Jesus Christ (1 Peter 1:3). As the apostle Paul said, we look "for the blessed hope and the appearing of the glory of our great God and Savior, Christ Jesus" (Titus 2:13).

As children of God, we are heirs of a boundless future. We have a future in heaven that fears no tomorrow because each day will be better than the last. This hope causes us to chime in with the apostle John, pleading, "Come, Lord Jesus" (Revelation 22:20).

Such hope offers comfort. With a calm composure, knowing of his imminent death at the guillotine, Evere'monde in *A Tale of Two Cities* said, "It is a far, far better rest that I go to, than I have ever known."[2]

Such hope looks to the future in triumph. When death seemed near for "Brother" in *The Pilgrim's Progress*, "Hopeful" said with excitement, "I see the gate, and men standing by to receive us."[3]

Death is near to us all. Our belief, our faith, our confidence, and our hope lie in what is to come because we belong to Jesus. And because we are His, we have no reason to fear anything—not even death. Paul the apostle wrote, "To die is to gain" (Philippians 1:21). Why? Because it is better "to be absent from the body and to be at home with the Lord" (2 Corinthians 5:8). For that reason the Word of God confirms, "O death, where is your sting?" (1 Corinthians 15:55).

John Bunyan (1628–1688), who wrote *The Pilgrim's Progress,* gave these last words at the end of his life: "Weep not for me, but for your-selves. I go to the Father of our Lord Jesus Christ, who will, through the mediation of His blessed Son, receive me, though a sinner, where I hope we shall meet to sing the new song, and remain everlastingly happy, world without end."[4]

William Wilberforce (1759–1833), an advocate for slaves, said to his family as he laid dying, "My affections are so much in heaven that I can leave you all without a regret; yet I do not love you less, but God more."[5]

Just moments before hymn writer Frances Havergal (1836–1879) died, she asked that the following Scripture verse be read to her: "I am the LORD, I have called you in righteousness, I will also hold you by the hand and watch over you" (Isaiah 42:6). With a smile on her face, Frances reflected over that verse and then said, "Called, held, kept! I can go to heaven on that!"[6]

All who are in Christ are indeed "called, held, kept"—in life and in death, on earth and in heaven. Wherever life leads us, we have the assur-ance of our salvation:

> *Even though I walk through the valley of the shadow of death, I fear no evil; for You are with me; Your rod and Your staff, they comfort me....Your have anointed my head with oil; my cup overflows. Surely goodness and lovingkindness will follow me all the days of my life, and I will dwell in the house of the LORD forever* (Psalm 23:4-6).

Notes

Chapter 1—The Promise of a Better Future

1. Nahum Mitchell, *History of the Early Settlement of Bridgewater, in Plymouth County, Massachusetts, Including an Extensive Family Register* (Boston: Kidder and Wright, 1840; repr. Bridgewater, MA: Henry T. Pratt, 1897; Baltimore: Gateway Press, 1970, 1975; Bowie, MD: Heritage Books, 1983).

2. Darrell S. Keith's article, "The Keiths and the Gunns," in the Clan Keith Society newsletter "Keith and Kin," found at http://the keithclan.com.

3. Ibid. My appreciation to Darrell S. Keith for his provision of facts, although I do calculate the length of the feud differently from Mr. Keith, who says the feud lasted 530 years.

4. John Wesley became born-again through the ministry of Moravian minister Count Nicholas Ludwig von Zinzendorf (1700–1760).

5. As cited at www.christianheroes.com/ev/ev022.asp.

6. As cited at www.christianheroes.com/ev/ev013.asp.

7. Help in trouble: Job 5:19; 8:20-21; Psalm 9:9; 18:2,28; 22:24; 31:23; 32:7; 34:19; 37:24,39; 42:11; 68:13; 71:20; 73:26; 91:10-11; 126:5-6; 138:7; 146:8; Lamentations 3:31-33; Micah 7:8-9; Nahum 1:7; John 16:33.

   Promises to the victim of slander: Job 5:21; Psalm 31:20; 37:6; 57:3; Isaiah 51:7.

8. "On the Death of Mr. Whitefield," sermon by John Wesley preached at the Chapel in Tottenham-Court Road and at the Tabernacle, near Moorfields on Sunday, November 18, 1770, as cited at http://gbgm-umbc.org/umhistory/wesley/sermons.

9. God's love: Deuteronomy 7:13; Psalm 146:8; Proverbs 15:9; Isaiah 62:5; Jeremiah 31:3; 32:41; Hosea 14:4; John 3:16; 16:27; 17:23,26; Ephesians 2:4-7; 2 Thessalonians 2:16-17; 1 John 4:10,16,19.

   God's protection: Psalm 4:8; 27:1; 91:9-10; 112:7; 121:7-8; Proverbs 1:33; 3:24; 18:10; Isaiah 43:1-2; Ezekiel 34:28.

   God's guidance: Psalm 32:8; 37:23; 48:14; 73:23-24; Proverbs 3:6; 11:5; 16:9; Isaiah 28:26; 30:21; 42:16.

   God's blessings: Proverbs 3:32-33; 10:3,22; 12:2; 15:16; 16:3,20; 19:14,17; 22:4; 25:21-22; 28:14,25; 30:7; 31:30.

10. Frederick W. Robertson, *Sermons* (New York: Harper & Brothers, n.d.), 311.

11. Proverbs 12:15; 13:16,20; 14:7,16; 17:7; 18:2; 20:3,19; 24:7; 26:1; 29:11; Ecclesiastes 2:14; 7:6; 10:3,14; 1 Corinthians 15:33.

12. Revelation 21:2 speaks of "the holy city, new Jerusalem, coming down out of heaven from God, made ready *as a bride adorned for her husband.*"

Chapter 2—The Promise of Protection and Strength

1. If you are interested in taking a look at this home, it's at 525 South Winchester Boulevard, San Jose, California 95128. To book a tour, you can call (408) 247-2101.

2. Grammatically, it would be more proper to say, "Vamos a morirnos."

3. Martin Luther and Katherine von Bora (married June 13, 1525) had six children, of whom three sons and one daughter survived them. When Lena, Luther's daughter, was being laid in her coffin, he said, "Darling Lena, you will rise and shine like a star, yea, like the sun....I am happy in spirit, but the flesh is sorrowful and will not be content, the parting grieves me beyond measure....I have sent a saint to heaven." Taken from Clyde L. Manschreck, editor, *A History of Christianity: The Church from the Reformation to the Present* (Grand Rapids, MI: Baker Book House, 1981), 2:51-52.

4. Taken from the following Scripture verses: Psalm 12:5; 91:14-16; 132:15; Isaiah 41:10; 45:2; Hebrews 13:5.

Chapter 3—The Promise of Provision for Your Every Need

1. John Newton, *Olney Hymns* (London: W. Oliver, 1779), BK1, hymn 36. The 1779 edition of the *Olney Hymns* can be found at Wheaton, IL: Christian Classics Ethereal Library, 1999-02, VO. 6, http://ccel.wheaton.edu/n/newton/olneyhymns/about.htm.

2. T. M. Lindsay, *Luther and the German Reformation* (Edinburgh: T. & T. Clark, 1900), 127.

Chapter 4—The Promise of an Everlasting Love

1. William Gesenius, *Gesenius' Hebrew and Chaldee Lexicon to the Old Testament, Translated with Additions and Corrections from the Author's Thesaurus and Other Works, by Samuel Prideaux Tregelles, LL.D.*, 1810-12, reprint (Grand Rapids, MI: Wm. B. Eerdmans, 1954.

2. I counted only the words that meant *hesed* (lovingkindness and lovingkindnesses), using Robert Thomas's *Exhaustive Concordance of the Bible* (La Habra, CA: The Lockman Foundation, 1981, 1998), 691.

3. Gesenius, 293.

4. R. Laird Harris, Gleason L. Archer, Jr., and Bruce K. Waltke, *Theological Wordbook of the Old Testament* (Chicago: Moody Press, 1980), 305.

5. Harris, 305.

6. Sarah F. Adams, "Nearer, My God, to Thee," found in *Great Hymns of the Faith* (Grand Rapids, MI: Zondervan, 1972), 357.

7. Charles Hodge, *Systematic Theology* (Grand Rapids, MI: Wm. B. Eerdmans, reprinted 1979), 1:429.

8. Ibid., 1:428.

9. G. Abbott-Smith, *A Manual Greek Lexicon of the New Testament* (Edinburgh: T. & T. Clark, 1921, 1954), 96.

10. Ibid.

11. Harris, Archer, and Waltke, *Theological Wordbook of the Old Testament*, 38. In regard to Hosea 2:16, the authors of *Theological Wordbook of the Old Testament* state on page 39: "The relationship of husband to wife is used as a metaphor of God's relationship to his people. This relationship is the basis of assurance of the people of God in the book of Hosea where the marriage relationship forms a central motif."

12. Donna Morley, poem titled *The Marriage Banquet*. The following verses inspired me as I wrote this poem: Jeremiah 31:3; Ephesians 2:8-9; Revelation 19:9; 21:2,25; 22:4.

13. Deuteronomy 7:13; Psalm 146:8; Proverbs 15:9; Isaiah 62:5; Jeremiah 31:3; Hosea 14:4; Zephaniah 3:17; John 3:16; 16:27; Ephesians 2:4-7; 2 Thessalonians 2:16-17; 1 John 4:10,16,19.

Chapter 5—Living Out Your Marriage Vow to Christ

1. The writer of this song is Samuel F. Smith, and the song was written in 1832. The composer was William Walker. The original song was called "The Missionary Farewell," found in Walker's *The Southern Harmony and Musical Companion* (Spartanburg, SC: William Walker, September 1835), 328. Some Mormons believe that in the 1850s a Mormon woman named Sally Masters wrote this *exact* song under the title "Yes, My Native Land I Love Thee." Yet all proof shows that Samuel F. Smith not only wrote this song in 1832, but that the song was placed in Walker's *Southern Harmony and Musical Companion* prior to it being placed in the hymnal of the Church of Jesus Christ of Latter-day Saints. See www.jackmasters.net/ raines.html.

2. John MacArthur, *The MacArthur Study Bible* (Nashville, TN: Word Publishing, 1997), 1439.

3. Joseph H. Thayer and William Smith, Greek lexicon entry for *chliaros*, *The KJV New Testament Greek Lexicon*, www.biblestudytools.net/Lexicons/Greek/grk.cgi? number=5513&version=kjv.

4. G. Abbott-Smith, *A Manual Greek Lexicon of the New Testament* (Edinburgh: T. & T. Clark, 1921, 1954), 287.

5. *The Valley of Vision* (Carlisle, PA: The Banner of Truth Trust, 1975), 122-23.

Chapter 6—Deepening the Relationship

1. Charles Neider, *ed., Great Shipwrecks and Castaways: Authentic Accounts of Disasters at Sea* (New York: Dorset Press, 1952, 1980), 196.
2. Ibid., 197.
3. Ibid., 201.
4. Ibid., 198.
5. Ibid., 199.
6. Ibid.
7. Ibid., 201.
8. Ibid., 200
9. Ibid., 201.
10. Ibid., 202.
11. Ibid.
12. Ibid.
13. Ibid., 203.
14. Ibid.
15. John Bunyan, *Grace Abounding to the Chief of Sinners* (London: George Larkin, 1666, 1765), Part 4, paragraph 206.
16. Ibid.
17. Neider, 201.
18. From A.M. Overton's poem "He Maketh No Mistakes." First printed in *The Brethren Evangelist,* and cited in Walter B. Knight's *Knight's Treasury of 2,000 Illustrations* (Grand Rapids, MI: Wm. B. Eerdmans, 1963), 332.

Chapter 7—Giving Him All Your Love

1. James C. Livingston, *Modern Christian Thought,* vol. 1, *The Enlightenment and the Nineteenth Century,* 2d ed. (Upper Saddle River, NJ: Prentice Hall, 1997), 31. Reimarus's work was published in seven fragments from 1774–78.
2. Helmut Thielicke, *Modern Faith and Thought* (Grand Rapids, MI: Wm. B. Eerdmans, 1990), 84.
3. Livingston, 30.
4. Ibid., 31.
5. Walter B. Knight, *Knight's Master Book of 4,000 Illustrations* (Grand Rapids, MI: Wm. B. Eerdmans, 1956), 390.

6. I had given Luwan my phone number so that I could connect her with other believers who were also Asian. Unfortunately, Luwan never called me, so I don't know if she started attending the church on her own, or if pressure from her parents kept her away. I firmly believe she was very sincere in wanting Jesus in her life and my hope is that she is now following Him.

7. Adapted from John MacArthur, *Matthew 16-23* (Chicago: Moody Press, 1988), 341.

Chapter 8—Experiencing Uninterrupted Joy

1. L.E. Maxwell, *Crowded to Christ* (Grand Rapids, MI: Wm. B. Eerdmans, 1952), 94.
2. Ibid.
3. Ibid.
4. Maurice Roberts, *The Thought of God* (Edinburgh: The Banner of Truth Trust, 1993), 130.
5. My trial ended in a way I never expected. The day before the scheduled surgery, the surgeon requested that I have one more CT scan (computerized tomography), also called a CAT scan (computerized axial tomography). What the surgeon found was amazing. The massive tumor on the right side of my brain was gone. Not even a hint of it could be detected. Both the surgeon and my doctor said, "We're completely dumbfounded!" While I was indeed stunned, I wasn't dumbfounded. I had prayed the Lord would heal me, but I had anticipated it would be through surgery. God obviously had a different plan. This surprise step by the Lord gave me yet another opportunity to share Christ with these men.

Chapter 9—Coveting His Love Letters

1. Sullivan Ballou died along with 27 of his close comrades and 4,000 other soldiers.
2. Civil War Series shown on PBS, 1990.
3. To read an array of love letters from the Civil War period, go to http://spec.lib.vt.edu/cwlove.
4. There was the intimidated Abram in Egypt (Genesis 12:10); Lot's hesitation to do as the angels urged (Genesis 19:16); the idle King David lusting on his rooftop (2 Samuel 11:2); the seduced "man of God" in the old prophet's house (1 Kings 13:19); the discouraged Elijah under a juniper tree (1 Kings 19:4); the disobedient Jonah in the belly of a sea creature (Jonah 2); and the miserable Peter, who had the boldness to go to Christ's trial but not bold enough to admit he was a disciple (Luke 22:55).
5. Noah's obedience led his family to dry land (Genesis 6–9); Joshua's trust in God's Word led him to victories in battle (Joshua 6 and 8); Ruth's devotion to her mother-in-law led her to the true God (Ruth 1:16); Mordecai's persistence and Esther's selflessness saved thousands of lives (Esther 4:14,16); the apostles' boldness in sharing the gospel brought Christianity to the uttermost part of the world;

and Paul's commitment to church planting built an early church (Acts 13:1-28,31).

6. Merrill C. Tenney, *Galatians: The Charter of Christian Liberty* (Grand Rapids, MI: Wm. B. Eerdmans, 1954), 189-190.

7. Donna Morley, poem titled *Going Back in Time*.

8. As cited at www.fatfree.com/archive/1997/mar/msg00384.html.

9. As cited at http://gingerbread.michaels.com/decoratingideas/gingerbreadnativity.cfm.

10. William Cowper, John Newton, and other hymnodists, *The Olney Hymns* (England: W. Oliver, 1779), book 1, hymn 3, 468. "Walking with God" by William Cowper. The 1779 edition of *The Olney Hymns* can be found at Wheaton, IL: Christian Classics Ethereal Library, 1999-02, v0.6 at http://ccel.wheaton.edu/n/newton/olney hymns/About.htm.

Chapter 10—Telling Others I Am His, He Is Mine

1. James Dobson, *Family News* (Colorado Springs: Focus on the Family, July 1998), 5-6.

2. Thomas Paine, *Age of Reason* (Luxembourg: Barlow Publishing, 1794, 1796), Part II, Section 20.

3. Ibid.

4. Corresponding to varying degrees of sin (Matthew 5:19,22-23; 23:23; Luke 12:47-48), there are also theological reasons to believe there are varying degrees of punishment both now and in eternity (Matthew 11:20-24; Luke 12:47-48).

5. G. Abbott-Smith, *A Manual Greek Lexicon of the New Testament* (Edinburgh: T. & T. Clark, 1921, 1954), 347.

6. Friederick W. Nietzsche, *The Antichrist*, trans. by Henry Louis Mencken (New York: Alfred A. Knopf, 1918), 39.

7. Scripture shows that right after Christ's death, the men started preparing for burial, and requested for the body of Jesus (John 19:38-40). We know this was done during daylight hours because Jesus died the ninth hour (Mark 15:25,34,37). This means He died at approximately 3:00 PM. See Ronald F. Youngblood, ed., *Nelson's New Illustrated Bible Dictionary* (Nashville: Thomas Nelson Publishers, 1995), 316.

8. Scripture states, "Joseph of Arimathea...asked Pilate that he might take away the body of Jesus; and Pilate granted permission. So he came and took away His body. Nicodemus... also came..." (John 19:38-39).

9. Marcus Tullius Cicero, *Orator* (De Oratore, 54 B.C.), 21.

10. Augustine, *On Christian Doctrine*, translated by Reverend Professor J. F. Shaw from *Select Library of Nicene and Post-Nicene Fathers* (Londonberry: 1886–1890), book 4, chapter 12, point 27.

11. Charles E. Prior, "I'll Go Where You Want Me to Go," *Great Hymns of the Faith* (Grand Rapids, MI: Zondervan Publishing, 1972), 440, second stanza.

Chapter 11—Enduring in Total Devotion

1. If you have a desire to jog, it's always best to have a physical checkup with your doctor first.

2. Additional race metaphors are found in Galatians 2:2; 5:7; Philippians 2:16; 1 Timothy 6:12; 2 Timothy 4:7; Hebrews 12:1-2.

3. *The Columbia Encyclopedia* (New York: Columbia University Press, 2001–2004), www.bartleby.com/65/.

4. We aren't saved by a race, but rather, by grace (Ephesians 2:8-9). If we "lose" the race, we don't lose our salvation. *We can't lose our salvation.* It's impossible (Romans 8:38-39; 2 Timothy 1:12). The question here is not about our salvation; it's about our spiritual life and our service to Jesus.

5. Additional references include Acts 9:1,13,21; 22:4,19; 26:10; 1 Corinthians 15:9; Galatians 1:13; Philippians 3:6; 1 Peter 1:13.

6. Revelation 19:8.

7. Matthew 25:21.

Do You Belong to Jesus?

1. The Lord Jesus had claimed His deity all throughout His ministry. Jesus discussed His deity with the Pharisees (Matthew 22:42-45) and with the rebellious Jews (John 8:58). Jesus also claimed certain attributes of deity, such as holiness (John 8:46), as well as omnipotence (all powerful) and omnipresence (ever present, John 11:11-14). Jesus did things only God can do, such as forgive sins (Mark 2:5-7), raise the dead (John 5:28-30; 11:43), and judge all men (John 5:22,27).

2. Charles Dickens, *A Tale of Two Cities* (New York: D.C. Heath & Co., Publishers, 1901), 366.

3. John Bunyan, *The Pilgrim's Progress* (Westwood, NJ: Barbour and Company, n.d.), 182.

4. Walter B. Knight, *Knight's Master Book of 4,000 Illustrations* (Grand Rapids, MI: Wm. B. Eerdman's Publishing Company, 1956), 158.

5. Ibid.

6. Ibid., 103.

About the Author

Prior to coming to the Lord, author Donna Morley pursued the study of dietetics and worked in the field for six years at two hospitals. Within her first year of becoming a Christian, the Lord completely changed her direction in life, giving her a desire to study God's Word, and eventually, to communicate that Word to others. She graduated from Logos Bible Institute and with honors from The Master's College with a degree in Christian Education.

As a women's ministry teacher, Donna builds women up in God's Word. She teaches in churches, at conferences, and as a guest in the college classroom. She speaks on a variety of spiritual-life topics as well as on the cults and non-Christian religions. She has also started and led evangelistic Bible studies. Drawing from her experiences of sharing Christ with people of various religious persuasions, she writes outreach materials that help Christian women introduce others to Jesus.

Donna and her husband Brian are the co-founders of Faith & Reason Forum, a ministry for those who want to think more deeply about God. Faith & Reason Forum challenges Christians to grow in their knowledge of the faith and nonbelievers to consider reasons for believing in the faith. For more information about the ministry, and for articles to uplift and challenge you in your faith, you can visit their website at

www.faithandreasonforum.com